Dedication...

Orange County Bounty is dedicated to our hard-working farm
families who grow the foods that nourish us, and preserve the views that feed our souls and
inspire our paintings!

This cookbook was inspired by Wallkill River School Chef and
artist Patricia Dunn, who provided a local foods banquet for our
plein air painting workshops. Her energy and enthusiasm provided
wings for this project.

Orange County Planner David Church was instrumental in getting
this book published. We are grateful for his help on this project, and
devotion to preserving Orange County's working farms and
agricultural heritage.

Acknowledgments....

Several people worked full time for many months to make this cookbook a reality. Here are the people behind the scenes alphabetized:

John Creagh is a demonstrating artist with the Wallkill River School and a professional graphic designer. He has taught both fine arts and graphic arts for many years. He applied his considerable talents to designing the cookbook, then many hours of eye-straining work laying out each page.

Shawn Dell Joyce is the Director of the Wallkill River School and was responsible for orchestrating this project. She juggled artists, farmers, and restaurants until all were able to meet on common ground. She generated master lists of farms that retail edibles and interfaced with the considerable amount of people and organizations that helped create this project.

Patricia Dunn is the Wallkill River School staff chef, and is responsible for getting this project started. She is the inspiration behind the cookbook, and a mixed media artist who has been painting with the Wallkill River School for many years. She has participated in many shows and competitions throughout the region.

Carrie Jacobson is an oil painter with the Wallkill River School and a newspaper editor. She used her magical wordsmithing ability to write the biographical pages about each farm and restaurant. She also applied her persuasive charm to restaurants to procure many of the recipes in this book.

Margaret Morales is a multi-media artist with the Wallkill River School and a practicing artist for 40 years. She is the techno-wiz behind the website and an organizer who generated many of the paintings and connections to farms and restaurants in this cookbook.

Pat Morgan is an amazing watercolorist who happened to own a bed and breakfast with her husband Richard. She is an excellent cook who took the raw recipes and typed them in a unified format for this cookbook. She also contributed many paintings and recipes from her own sizable collections as well as from her wide circle of friends.

Orange County Tourism Director **Susan Cayea** has contributed much time, material, many recipes and resources to this cookbook project.

Royal Fireworks Press publisher **Dr. Tom Kemnitz** made this book a reality. Without his help and hard work, we would not have been able to publish the book on the shoestring budget we fundraised.

"The following organizations contributed financially and/or worked to make the cookbook a success..."

Agricultural and Farmland Protection Board (AFPB). The *AFPB* works in a variety of ways to support the continuation of agriculture and the preservation of farmland. The Board's organization and membership is set by New York State statute. Board members include farmers and agri business entrepreneurs joined by the County Commissioner of Planning, and the County Director of Real Property along with a representative of the Orange County Legislature, of Cornell Cooperative Extension, and of the County Soil and Water Conservation District. To learn more about the good work of this board, visit **www.orangecountygov.com,** click *"Planning"* then *"Agriculture."*

ShopRite and *Wakefern Corporation* contributed greatly to the printing costs of this book. *ShopRite* has a corporate headquarters in Florida, NY, and is featuring local produce in many of its store's produce aisles. Look for special *"Local"* signs on produce displays. *ShopRite* also offers cooking workshops with Executive Chef Faith Alahverdian. Look for the cooking class schedule in stores and for special book signing tables for *Orange County Bounty* in your *ShopRite*. See the back of the book for a listing of area *ShopRite* stores.

Orange County Tourism office generously supplied many recipes from its recent "Farmers' Market Recipe Contest." *O.C. Tourism* also allowed us to use much of its historic trivia which you will find in orange boxes throughout the book. Additionally, many employees including Director Susan Cayea include their personal favorite recipes for your enjoyment. See *Orange County Tourism's* page in the back of the book for more information about the office's fine programming and Orange Arts information.

Cornell Cooperative Extension is a small group of dedicated people who run programs like 4-H, Agricultural support programs, Master Gardener Programs, gleaning fresh produce for food banks, nutrition and health, environment, community development, and other programs. C.C.E. generously shared its farmers' markets lists, and helped us generate a master list of farms that retail edibles in Orange County. Many individuals were particularly key to the book like Stiles Najac who visited restaurants with us to help collect recipes, Marie Ullrich, Lucy Joyce, Rose Baglia, and Darlene Price all helped with the cookbook, as did many others behind the scenes. **www.cce.cornell.edu**

Wallkill River School is an artist-owned nonprofit arts organization that spent about a year working on this project. The entire school contributed to the cookbook by visiting every restaurant we could find in Orange County that may use local produce. There is no list of such places, so we had to make our own by asking our local farmers, and visiting eateries in our hometowns. Every effort was made by volunteer artists to contact all the restaurants and farms in Orange County. Some slipped through the cracks and we hope to find them for the second printing. A good deal of funding for the cookbook came from financial contributions from these restaurants and farms. We could not have printed this book without their help.

Scenic FOOD

Gourmet BEAUTY

We have all the right ingredients.

Get a taste of our farm markets and wineries. Our local chefs will tickle your palate while our festivals tickle your fancy. And there are so many other delicious things to see and do in Orange County, New York.

Call us or just click on our website. We'll tell you more.

800-762-8687

WWW.ORANGETOURISM.ORG

Following in the tradition of our ancestors in the Hudson River School, the artists of the *Wallkill River School* draw attention to diminishing open spaces and the need to preserve them. The nonprofit collective offers a variety of artistic and educational opportunities for artists and audiences. We provide a "hands on" art experience for diverse populations from children to seniors. We foster a connection between artists and the land that sustains us. The artists in the school often initiate special projects and auction their work in benefit auctions to raise money for nonprofits who help preserve our open spaces and agricultural heritage.

THE WALLKILL RIVER SCHOOL

The *Wallkill River School* offers plein air (outdoors) painting workshops on Orange County farms, open spaces, and historic sites from May through October. These workshops feature local demonstrating artists, personal instruction, group critique and a local foods lunch. All workshops are handicapped accessible, have a restroom available, and an on-site babysitter upon request. These workshops happen in six different locations, but always on Sundays from 9am-noon.

From November through May, the *WRS* operates atelier-style classes on Sunday with a staff instructor leading still life, figure drawing and floral painting classes from 9am-noon. Other workshops are offered during the year at the *WRS* geared toward absolute beginners, advanced, intermediate and professional artists. Most workshops are taught by the finest artists in Orange County, with special "drop in" workshops for seniors on Tuesday mornings from 10am-noon.

The *WRS* also partners with local Bed and Breakfasts to offer weekend art workshop packages featuring national-level workshop instructors from around the country. Weekend Get-away Workshops include meals at Montgomery's finest local restaurants, a two-night three-day stay in an historic home, art instruction, and a little extra time for antiquing and sight-seeing in the historic Village of Montgomery.

The *WRS* runs an after school arts program for children from 3:30-5:30pm every school day, and a summer arts camp program at Benedict Town Park during July. Each after school workshop features a different art skill including clay, cartooning, drawing with an artist's eyes, sculpture from natural materials and turning reusable materials into art.

The *Wallkill River School* gallery represents the artwork of the workshop instructors and others specializing in plein air painting in our area. The gallery is free and open to the public from 10am-7pm Tues.-Sun. Opening receptions always the second Saturday of each month from 5-8pm and and feature a live demonstration by the exhibiting artists.

For a complete class schedule visit **www.WallkillRiverSchool.com** or stop by the *Wallkill River School* at 100 Ward St. in Montgomery, at the intersection of route 17K and 211. **(845) 457-ARTS**

Be a Localvore

By Shawn Dell Joyce (reprinted from the Times Herald Record)

A sadly unappetizing fact about our food is it travels further than most of us do every year. The average bite of food on an American plate traveled 1500-2500 miles, on a journey that took between 7 to14 days to make it from the farm to your mouth. In order to survive that long journey, many fruits are picked while hard and green, and then sprayed with a hormone to help them ripen. This is just one of the unnatural practices that has become perfectly natural in our industrialized food system.

More calories were used in fossil fuels to transport that food than it will provide your body in nutrition. On its journey, it passed through the hands of growers, pickers, packers, shippers, middlemen, dock workers, clerks, stores, each one taking their little bite of the purchase price. Even though you probably paid a hefty price, our farmers only received an average of 6 cents from every dollar paid for their produce. The costs to the environment to mass produce that food item, store, chill, transport and market it are enormous. Even if you scrub it with a stiff brush, you won't wash off all that bad karma.

What's a caring consumer to do about the loss of small family farms, food security, and seasonal eating? Become a "localvore" even if you are already an omnivore or an herbivore. Localvores are folks who eat what is grown in their region, usually within a 100 mile radius. Many New England states have adopted and promoted being localvore. Vermont and New Hampshire both have extensive localvore groups who produce cookbooks and meet for local-grown potlucks. Some communities in this region have taken the "Localvore Challenge" where organizers promote eating local, stores sell local produce, and restaurants offer local food dishes for a week to a month.

While becoming a localvore may sound too close to tree hugging for some people consider this; try buying 10% of your fruits and vegetables locally. If we all did this simple act it would save more than 300,000 gallons of fossil fuel and keep up to 9 million pounds of CO_2 from being emitted. It is also more pleasurable because local foods are picked in season and ripe, so they taste better.

Every dollar we spend on food is a vote either for preserving our local farms and food security, or for the big agro-industry and their environmentally destructive practices.

Marcia Passos Duffy, publisher of The Heart of New England weekly newsletter says; "This week while at your supermarket, try buying one or two products that come from your local area. Or visit your local farmers' market. It's these small choices made everyday by people like you and me that can tip the scales in favor our rural heritage and can save family farms from being plowed under into yet another strip mall."

www.slowfoodusa.org • www.100milediet.org • www.localharvest.org

Orange County Bounty Cookbook

Spring

(April, May, June)

What's in season?

Fruits

    Apples (from last fall until June)

    Sweet Cherries (late June)

    Strawberries (Late May through June)

Vegetables

    Asparagus (Mid May-Mid June)

    Beets (Late June)

    Broccoli (June)

    Cabbage (Mid June)

    Herbs (Cilantro, Parsley, Rosemary, Thyme)

Lettuce (Mid May)

Peas (late June)

Radishes (May)

Rhubarb (Mid May)

Spinach (Mid May)

Squash Blossoms (May)

Squash (Late June)

Meats

Lamb

Honey

Eggs

Shawangunk Growers
Mount Hope
(845) 775-6825
http://gunkhort.com/home.html

"Tall Flowers", by Pat Morgan.

Rachel Doty of Shawangunk Growers and Horticultural Service says she loves being a farmer.

She and her husband, Ed, along with baby son Isaac, have been in business in Mount Hope since 2005. They sell quality plants at local farmers' markets. Rachel says they often have plants that are hard to find elsewhere in the region. They're also happy to give gardening advice!

Collecting and growing plants for over two decades, Ed and Rachel have extensive growing experience. They've responded to the need to offer deer-resistant, unusual, native, rare, and new varieties of perennials and annuals.

The trend of eating locally is tremendously important, Rachel says. Among other things, it helps support the local farms and farmers.

Shawangunk Horticultural Service, a specialty landscape design service, offers custom design, installation, maintenance and consultation. They use new and hardy varieties of plants, shrubs, and trees, and have maintained several gardens featured in recent local garden tours.

The horticultural service also volunteered the design and installation of Warwick Sandfordville Elementary School's Peace Memorial Garden.
http://peacewallmemorial.org/contributors

Gardening is a healthy hobby, the Doty's believe, that helps relieve stress. When the world is too much, too fast, too busy, too technological, time spent in the garden, with your hands in the earth, can calm anyone, physically and mentally.

"We are very sincere in our effort to produce healthy flowers and herbs for everyone to enjoy," Rachel says.

Bounty Cookbook

EDIBLE FLOWER SALAD
(courtesy of Rachel Doty)

Ingredients: Nastertiums, pansies, calendula
history or origins of this recipe : unknown
recipe : 1/2 cp of nasturtiums
1/2 cp of pansies
1/2 cp of calendula
2 cloves of garlic diced
1/2 lb of baby greens mixed
one sliced medium size tomato
5 sliced radishes
two stalsks of celery diced
1/2 purple onion diced
1/2 chopped sweet red pepper
1/2 chopped green pepper

"Blue Flowers", by Pat Morgan.

Toss gently and allow each person at the table to put their own
dressing. Best with Honey mustard dressing.. Yield 5 to 6 servings

*"The highest point in Orange County is
Schunnemunk Mountain at nearly 1700 feet.
It is one of New York's newest state parks with an 8-mile long
open ridge offering expansive views of the Hudson Highlands,
Shawangunks, Catskills, and Hudson River."*

Pat Morgan, a watercolor painter, has studied with artists including Richard Ochs, Eli Rosenthal and Mel Stabin. Currently, she is represented by the Wallkill River Gallery. She has received local and regional awards for her work, and enjoys teaching other painters her love of watercolor.

Blooming Hills Farms
1251 Rt. 208
Blooming Grove, NY

Cornwall Farm Stand
Otterkill Rd.
Mountainville, NY
(845) 782-7310
www.bloominghillfarm.com

"Orange County Bounty", Pastel by Mary Sealfon.

On the home page of Blooming Hill Farm's website is a line that says it all: "Don't buy food from strangers."

Blooming Hill is, in 2007, in its 26th year of farming in the Hudson Valley. The farm has struggled to survive "with all the ecologic and economic realities of an organic family farm."

It's done so by diversifying crops, diversifying its marketing effort, and diversifying its customer base.

Community Supported Agriculture, or CSA, helps Blooming Hill and other local farms. People buy shares at the start of the season, and have fresh produce for the year. CSAs help farmers stabilize their income, and let community members have the freshest produce at a discount.

"It is our hope," Blooming Hill says, "to show current and future generations the importance of locally produced food and the place which working farms have in the landscape of today and tomorrow."

At its farm in Blooming Grove and its farm stand in Mountainviille, Blooming Hill offers fruits, vegetables, preserves, honey, cheese, breads, herbs and more. Also available are lessons and lectures on organic farming, artisan and craft demonstrations and good stuff to eat.

Plum Point was the first European settlement in Orange County. Col. Patrick MacGregorie created a trading post at the site in 1685. It operated until 1720.

Bounty Cookbook

BRAISED GREENS WITH LOTS OF GARLIC
(Recipes courtesy of Marge Corriere,
Blooming Hills Farms)

"Farm Truck, " Oil by William Noonan.

1 lb kale, mustard greens, or chard
1-2 Tbsp e v olive oil
5 cloves garlic, minced
salt and pepper to taste, fresh lemon

Wash greens thoroughly, and chop into small pieces. Heat oil in a large skillet and sauté garlic for two minutes. Add wet greens to skillet, no need to add water. Cover and cook over medium heat for about 10 minutes, stirring occasionally to coat all greens with the garlic and oil. Serve with lemon wedges. Yield 4 servings

HERB VINIAGRETTE

3 TB. fresh lemon juice
1 TB. balsamic vinegar
3 TB. olive oil
3 TB. finely minced shallots (about 1 large)
2 TB. minced fresh parsley
2 TB. thinly sliced fresh basil
1 tsp. minced fresh oregano, or dill, or other herb

Blend together, let sit for about 1/2 hour. Add to any fresh green salad. Slice raw summer squash, green beans, onion, carrot, etc. into the salad.

Mary Mugele Sealfon received a BA in painting at the U of California at Santa Barbara and a MA from NYU. In New York City she pursued a career as an Art Director and designer. She has won numerous awards and her paintings and prints have been exhibited nationally and internationally. She also teaches art locally, including SUNY Orange.

William Noonan is an artist who resides and works in Orange County. He is known for his loose brushwork and sophisticated use of color. You can see examples of his work on his website at www.williamnoonan.com.

Orange County

Hall Gorta

Hal Gorta was a vibrant young artist and activist who specialized in Trompe L'Oeil images and traditional realism. He was a demonstrating artist for the Wallkill River School, and community activist in Pine Bush and Newburgh. He died unexpectedly in 2006 leaving a legacy of award-winning paintings and broken-hearted friends.

"Grapes" by Hall Gorta

"New Windsor Opera Star Claudia Cummings has sung leading roles including those in Lucia, La Traviata, Die Fledermaus, The Marriage of Figaro, Don Giovanni, Lulu, and The Tales of Hoffman in opera houses in New York City, Chicago, San Francisco, Seattle, San Diego, Miami, Toronto, Amsterdam, and Stuttgart, and is married to Shakespearian actor Jack Aranson."

Bounty Cookbook

VEGAN SPANAKOPITA ROLLS
(courtesy of Hal Gorta)

1 large bag fresh organic spinach
organic buttery spread (Earth Balance)
3 cloves garlic- quartered
1 package (approx.1 lb.) organic frozen fillo dough (The Fillo Factory)
Vegan cheese- mozzarella/monterey jack (Vegan Gourmet)
Sea salt

Defrost fillo dough in refrigerator for a few hours. This allows the dough to defrost slowly- dough will be less sticky and easier to handle than defrosting in room temperature.

Rinse spinach well and soak in cold water. Shake or spin dry when ready to use. Stuff 1/3 spinach and one clove garlic in food processor. Use pulse function and chop- off and on- just until spinach is all chopped. Empty into large bowl. Repeat twice more with the remaining spinach and garlic. Add sea salt to taste- about 1 tbsp. to start.

Unroll defrosted fillo dough on smooth surface dusted lightly with some organic flour. Warm about 6-8 ounces buttery spread until melted- remove from heat.

Take one sheet of fillo dough carefully from one corner, keeping it in one piece and place on another flour dusted surface. Using a 1 inch paint brush (new) lightly coat fillo sheet with melted buttery spread. Repeat with additional sheets, lying one on top of the other, until there are 4 layers.

After coating the 4th sheet, spoon a third of the spinach/garlic mixture, one to two inches from the end of one of the shorter sides. Slice some vegan cheese and lie on top of mixture. Fold layered fillo around the spinach into a roll. Coat roll lightly with the melted buttery spread. Cut roll in half and place, loose side down, into 13x9inch buttered baking pan. Repeat with all six rolls.

Bake at 300degreesF for 15 minutes and broil an additional 15 minutes at the same temperature- or until lightly brown. Cut into quarters for hors d'ouerves, or as is for meal. Yield 4 servings

Applewood Orchards
Warwick, NY
(845) 986-1684
www.applewoodorchards.com

"Applewood Orchards", by Mary Sealfon.

The Hull family knows that farming is a tough job. The days are long, the tasks are difficult, and you can be a victim of everything from bugs to weather to fire.

The challenges go even farther than that, though. To be successful, David and Susanna Hull say, you've got to be an agronomist, climatologist, entomologist, mechanic, biologist and chemist. But, they say,

"We love owning our own business."

David Hull's father bought 100 acres in the Warwick Valley in 1949. The next year, David began planting apple trees. Five years later, Hull turned to orcharding full-time.

In 1971, with the orchard going full-swing, the Hulls' storage facility burned down, with that year's crop inside it. The next year, Applewood opened a pick-your-own business. The orchard's storage needs were reduced, the people were happy, and the fruit was on its way.

Hull's son, Jonathan, started the winery in 1997. The wine is fermented, bottled, and sold at the Winery and is valued for its rich bouquet, full body, and fragrant aroma.

The Hulls believe that there is a great bounty of food in the county and "we should all enjoy it." Eating local helps the farmer financially, and that saves open space and farmland.

"Eating locally is one step toward healthier food for the family," they say, adding that eating food grown in our county ties us to our county. "It helps to make us all the more community-connected," the Hulls say.

Their spacious farm has 122 acres of rolling hills to walk through and picnic in, award-winning herb and flower gardens to stroll by and farm animals to pet and enjoy. People can have their weddings there. The shops sell wine and gifts, along with produce, and delicious apple cider, donuts, pies and luncheons.

Bounty Cookbook

SHORT RIB RAGU
(courtesy of Applewood Orchards)

4 lbs. short ribs, cut flanken style across the ribs into 2 inch pieces
salt and freshly ground pepper • 2 TB. vegetable oil • 1 dried bay leaf
2 sprigs fresh rosemary • 5 sprigs fresh thyme • 4 sprigs fresh flat-leaf parsley
4 carrots, diced • 2 celery stalks, diced • 1 medium onion, diced • 2 shallots, diced
1 TB. flour • 2 TB. tomato paste • 1/2 c. Applewood's Ruby's Kiss wine
2 c. Applewood's Merlot • 6 cloves garlic, peeled and smashed • 3-1/2 c. beef broth
1 pound pasta such as pappardelle or large rigatoni
chopped parsley and grated Pecorino Romano for garnish

Preheat oven to 325. Season the short ribs generously with salt and pepper. Place a large casserole or Dutch oven over medium heat. Add oil and heat until almost smoking. Add short ribs in batches and brown on all sides. Transfer to a large bowl and set aside.

Prepare bouquet garni: Place bay leaf, rosemary, thyme and parsley in a piece of cheesecloth and tie up with kitchen string. Set aside.

When ribs are cooked, add carrots, celery, onion and shallot to oil remaining in casserole. Cook over medium heat stirring occasionally, until softened and golden, about 10 minutes. Add the flour and tomato paste to the casserole and stir to combine. Add Ruby's Kiss and stir with a wooden spoon, scraping up all the browned bits from the pan. Add the Merlot and simmer until reduced by half. Add the garlic, beef broth and bouquet garni. Return the ribs to the casserole and stir to combine. Bring to a simmer over medium0high heat. Cover and place in the preheated oven. Cook until ribs are very tender and the meat is falling off the bones, about 3 hours.

Remove ribs to the casserole and place in a large bowl. When ribs are cool enough to handle, remove the meat from the bones and shred into bite size pieces. Degrease the sauce and discard the bouquet garni. Return the meat to pan and simmer to reduce to desired thickness. Serve over desired pasta, garnished with parsley and grated Romano. Yield 4 servings

Mary Mugele Sealfon received a BA in painting at the U of California at Santa Barbara and a MA from NYU. In New York City she pursued a career as an Art Director and designer. She has won numerous awards and her paintings and prints have been exhibited nationally and internationally. She also teaches art locally, including SUNY Orange.

Rogowski Farms
Warwick, NY
(845) 258-4574
www.rogowskifarm.net

"Black Dirt Pickers", watercolor by John Creagh.

Rogowoski Farm is a second generation family farm located in the black dirt region of Pine Island. What began as a 10 1/2-acre venture in 1955 has grown to a diverse operation, growing more than 250 varieties of produce each year on more than 150 acres. Its ecologically friendly and environmentally sound agricultural practices combine with progressive attitudes and family values to create an atmosphere of warmth and welcome.

Rogowski Farm, which proclaims itself the only Certified Naturally Grown farm in the Town of Warwick, is known for custom-growing special ethnic varieties of produce for CSA clients and farmers' markets, and hopes to expand this service. The farm's special interests include heirloom tomatoes and other plants, sown from seeds handed down for generations. In addition to Rogowski produce, the farm store sells products, including hydroponic tomatoes, peppers and cucumbers, from many other farms in the region.

Community Supported Agriculture
2007 marks their ninth year of CSA farming. Cheryl Rogowski, taking over from her dad, converted the onion farm into a CSA that supports many families, farmers' markets, and seniors in the region. Cheryl also has her own radio show on WTBQ, and is an activist-farmer who won the MacArthur Fellowship (genius award) in 2001 for her sustainability activism. Beginning in 1999 with 12 customers their client base has grown to 156 members. This client base has grown solely by word of mouth as a result of the high quality of service and product they offer.

"The Black Dirt region in Pine Island
is the "Onion Capitol of the World."

Bounty Cookbook

GREEN GARLIC MASHED POTATOES
(courtesy of Rogowski Farms)

1 1/2 pounds potatoes
4 tablespoons butter
1/2 cup minced green garlic, use the white and pale green parts only
1/2 cup milk
1/2 cup cream
Salt and freshly ground pepper to taste

"Garlic" by Ann Marie Nitti.

Peel and cut the potatoes. Place in a large saucepan with enough salted water to cover by several inches. Bring to a simmer, cover and adjust heat to maintain a gentle simmer. Cooking the potatoes just until tender. Depending on the variety of potatoes used it could take about 30 minutes. Test with a knife or fork - when it will slip in easily they are done. Drain, and return the potatoes to the warm pot. Return the pot to the heat and shake it until any moisture remaining evaporates.

While the potatoes are cooking, melt the butter in a small saucepan over moderate heat. Add the green garlic and sauté until softened, 3 to 5 minutes, until translucent but not brown. Add the milk and cream. Season to taste with salt and pepper.

Mash the potatoes with a food mill or ricer. Add the hot milk mixture and stir vigorously with a wooden spoon until smooth. Taste and adjust seasoning as needed. Yield 6 servings

*"Orange County has over 52 farms
that retail edibles directly to
Orange County residents."*

John Creagh has been a painter and an instuctor for over 25 years, as well as a member and instructor for the Wallkill River School. His artwork is featured in many private colections around the world, you can visit him at www.jcreagh.com

Ann Marie Nitti is an illustrator, designer and instructor, who is certified in watercolor/Botanical Art by the New York Botanical Gardens. www.allcustomart.com

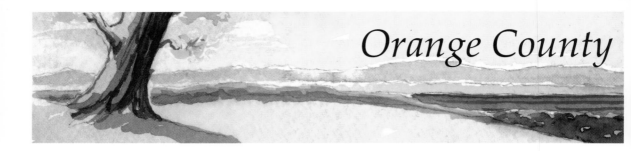

Bellvale Farms
5 Bellvale Lakes Road
Warwick, NY 10990
 (845) 988-5414

Creamery: 385 Route 17A
(845) 988-1818
www.bellvalefarms.com

"Bellvale Farms" by Michelle Filer

In the Town of Warwick, Bellvale Farms - well, its cows - has produced milk for more than 150 years. The farm's history dates back to 1819, when Willam Wisner bought land from William Noble.

Over the years, Bellvale bought adjoining land, until the farm grew to 450 acres. Good soil and plenty of rain have helped produce tasty grass and quality hay, and that makes for happy and productive cows, and happy and productive farmers. Over the years, the farm has sold milk for drinking, making cheese, and for producing butter and ice cream. Bellvale Farms itself has added a creamery, featuring homemade ice cream.

The best part of the farming life, says Amy Noteboom, is "the stories of farming shared between the generations on our farm. My husband and father answer questions about what farming was like when they were the ages of my children."

Eating locally makes sense on lots of levels, Noteboom says. One primary one is food safety. You can drive to the farm. You can look at it, see how clean it is, how careful the farmer is. "Chances are if the farm is clean the produce or products are also."

Noteboom's ancestors have farmed these same fields since the early 1800s. There is a commitment there, a memory, a history, a hope. Members of the fifth and sixth generation own and run the farm these days, and the seventh generation already is helping out.

"All the family members live and work on our farm," Noteboom says. "We are dedicated to improving the land and protecting our limited water below. Each generation has inherited a beautiful place to work, live and raise a family. I want to ensure future generations will have the same history to share with their children."

Bounty Cookbook

"OUR MILK"
(courtesy of Bellvale Farms Creamery)

This recipe has been passed down from generation to generation for almost 200 years

40 lbs corn silage (including entire corn, plant ear and kernels)

25 lbs alfalfa haylage

33lbs of grains including soybean, barley, oats, cornmeal and minerals and salt

21 lbs dried alfalfa hay

"Buckbee Farm (Bellvale Farm Creamery)" by Michelle Filer

Mix and serve to one Holstein Cow. Add 35 gallons of water. Provide a comfortable, cool place to live. Wait a little while, then see what you can get from the other end by milking the cow. Chill and serve. Yield 80 people one 12 ounce serving.

"Claudius Smith, a famous outlaw and British loyalist was hung in Goshen during the Revolutionary War. He is said to be buried in the old Presbyterian Church. His stolen treasures are still hidden in the hills around Goshen."

Michelle Filer is a student of the Wallkill River School. She is married to her best friend, Dan, and together they are raising two amazing and beautiful little girls, both of whom are little artists in their own right. Michelle knows that life is good and is proud to paint in the Hudson Valley.

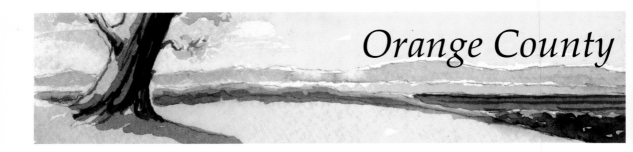

Lawrence Farms
Newburgh, NY
(845) 562-4268

"Lawrence Farms Orchard" , by Jane Lawrence

One of the most popular destinations in Orange County is Lawrence Farms Orchards. The farm has been doing a "Pick Your Own" fruits and vegetables program for over 30 years. This family-owned and operated farm was established by the Lawrence's great-grandfather in 1892, who emigrated from England. Now there are three generations of Lawrence's working the farm.

The farm is nestled at the base of the ridge with scenic vistas and a "Little Village" and hay bale maze. The quaint "Little Village" is reminiscent of an old-fashioned New England farm town. Customers enjoy its charm as they are carried away to that simpler time and place of long ago. Customers can also be literally carried away by the horse-drawn carriage (weekends only). While enjoying a relaxing ride around the farm, you can nibble home-made doughnuts and local dairy farm ice cream.

The farm also sports "show chickens", playful goats, and a "friendly family atmosphere." In the winter, guests enjoy hot chocolate or coffee as they pick out their holiday trees. The farm is all decked out for the holidays, and the little village is lit up festively. Gift baskets are available for the holidays filled with farm produce and products. The bakery offers fresh-baked pies, homemade doughnuts, cookies, breads, and muffins.

Bounty Cookbook

FRESH STRAWBERRY PIE
(courtesy of Lawrence Farms Orchards)

Will need 2-1/2 – 3 quarts of strawberries and one 8" pie crust.

3 c. crushes strawberries
3 rounded TB cornstarch
3/4 c. sugar

Mix together. Bring this mixture to a boil and cook, stirring constantly, for 8-10 minutes. Let cool. Fill baked pie crust half full with sliced, raw strawberries. Pour half of the cooled glaze mixture over the raw berries in the crust, add more raw, sliced berries and top with the rest of the glaze mixture. Chill and serve with whipped cream.

Low Fat Pie Crust:
2 c. flour
1 tsp. salt
1/2 c. cooking oil
1/4 c. water

Mix together to form dough ball. Do not knead or mix too much. Roll out on floured surface. Place in pie dish and, with a fork, poke holes on bottom and sides of crust to prevent air pockets. Bake at 375 until crust turns golden. Let cook before filling.
Yield 6 servings

"America's smallest forest has only one tree, an Eastern Cottonwood that is 302 years old. The Balmville Tree, outside of Newburgh, is on the National Register of Historic Places as well as the New York State Register."

Jane Lawrence has been working as an artist for over 30 years, and focusing on pastel for the past 10 years. She is part of the husband and wife farmer team that has kept Lawrence Farms a popular destination.

Bounty Cookbook

RHUBARB & STRAWBERRY PIE
(courtesy of Evelyn Maier Joyce)

Rhubarb filling:
2c. rhubarb (diced) available locally in spring farmer's markets
2c. strawberries (sliced)
1c. sugar
3TBS. cornstarch
1/8 tsp. salt
Pie Crust:
Combine all ingredients above in a bowl and set aside while you make the crust.
2c. flour (sifted)
1/4 tsp. salt
2/3 c. shortening
4-6 TBS. cold water

"Grandma's Hands" by Shawn Dell Joyce

Sift flour and salt together. Cut in shortening with pastry blender or two knives. Add water a TBS. at a time until the mixture holds together. Divide dough into two parts. Roll out dough onto floured board to desired size. Line a pie pan , being careful not to stretch the dough. Place filling in pie pan. Roll out remaining dough, and lay over filled pie shell. Create a lattice design by cutting the top crust in strips and weaving it together. Press edges with a fork to seal. Bake at 425 degrees for 10 minutes, then reduce to 350 degrees for 20 minutes. Makes one delicious pie!

Shawn Dell Joyce is a sustainable artist and activist, founder of the Wallkill River School, and writes a syndicated weekly column called "Sustainable Living" in the Sunday Times Herald Record. She has works in major museum collections, and private collections around the world. www.WallkillRiverSchool.com

Bounty Cookbook

SAUTEED CHARD AND COLLARDS WITH WHITE BEANS
(courtesy of Liana Hoodes and Dave Church)

1 can White beans (navy or cannelloni)
Olive oil (although our daughter Ali who now lives in the almost South (Baltimore), says that it's best with bacon fat)
Onion diced
2-4 cloves garlic, chopped (garlic lovers can even use more!)
1 bunch swiss chard
1 bunch collards
1 jalapeno, minced (optional)
Salt and pepper to taste

Lightly saute diced onion in oil until translucent

Clean greens and separate stems from the greens. Chop Chard and Collard stems and add to cooking onions. Coarsely chop greens and add with chopped garlic and diced jalepeno. Season with salt, and lots of fresh black pepper. Add 1-2 TBS water if needed, stir, cover, and cook until greens reduce. Add White beans until heated through and serve over rice or pasta.

VARIATIONS:
Add chopped hot or sweet Italian sausage (uncooked, add with onions; or use leftover sausage and add later to heat) or add baby shrimp, and season with cilantro.
Freeze in quart freezer bags and add to chicken soup in the winter

"Baseball legend Babe Ruth often visited
the America House Hotel in Chester,
leaving a legacy of memories for local boys
who played baseball in Chester's fields and lots."

Bounty Cookbook

SPINACH RECIPE (IRRESISTIBLE SPRING DISH)
(courtesy of Barbara Vaughan)

2 lbs. fresh farmer's market spinach, rinsed and trimmed
10 ozs. fresh mushrooms, sliced thinly
1/2 lb. fresh bean sprouts
1/4 c. sesame oil
1/2 c. soy sauce

Blanche the bean sprouts in boiling water for 2 minutes. Rinse with cool water three times to remove bitterness. Toss with trimmed spinach, soy sauce and sesame oil. Eat immediately.

"Barbara Vaughan" by Shawn Dell Joyce

HOT BACON DRESSING (for Spinach Salad)
(courtesy of Denise Heude)

3 slices bacon
1 tablespoon flour
2 tablespoon sugar
1 egg, beaten
1/4 cup vinegar
1 cup water

Cut bacon into small pieces, fry until crisp. Remove bacon from drippings. Mix flour with sugar. Add egg, vinegar and water to flour and sugar mixture. Stir till well blended. Pour into drippings. Cook until thickened. Pour over spinach and/or other garden greens. Garnish with bacon bits and hard boiled eggs.

OVEN BAKED WHOLE WHEAT RASPBERRY PANCAKES
(courtesy of Warwick Valley Bed and Breakfast)

"Fresh Eggs" by Michelle Filer.

2 cups whole wheat flour
1/2 cup natural sugar
1 teaspoon baking soda
1 teaspoon baking powder
2 tablespoons canola oil
2 eggs
1 cup raspberries
1-1/2 cup fat free milk

Mix dry ingredients well; add oil, eggs, and milk slowly for consistency a little thicker than yogurt. Fold in raspberries.

Use two pie dishes. Melt a small amount of butter in each and then divide the batter in two. Bake on middle shelf for about 30 minutes at 350 degrees; rotate after 15 minutes.

Slice like pie and sprinkle a small amount of confectioner's sugar with a drizzle of maple syrup for garnish (a couple of raspberries optional).

Variations: seasonal fruit instead of raspberries and 1-1/2 cup white flour, 1/4 cups oats, 1/4 cup ground flax meal instead of 2 cups whole wheat flour

"Florida boasts the "Polka King";
Jimmy Sturr who has won 16 Grammys,
been nominated for 22."

Borden Farm

By Kenneth Hasbrouck,
1955 courtesy of the Historical Society of
Shawangunk and Gardiner

"3 Cows" by Eileen Piasecki-Couch

The Borden Home Farm was a small village unto itself. John Borden came to Wallkill in 1881 and started the condensery. He purchased the J.P. Andrews place (originally Benjamin Hasbrouck farm). The old stone house (still standing) was added to by the Andrews and John Borden. Other farms adjoining the first purchase were bought and the Borden holdings totaled about two thousand acres. Mr. Borden kept accurate records of all the farm's former owners and deeds.

Mr. Borden built the famous circular barn, which was later torn down and divided up. It was very large with a barnyard in the center. The long barn (still standing) was built about the same time. When Mr. Borden first made his home in Wallkill, there were two stone houses on the hill. The oldest one stood where Miss Marion Borden built the mansion in 1906. After John Borden's death in 1891, his wife continued to run the estate. Mr. Martin DeWitt was secretary to the Bordens from 1902-1930. At that time he took over the management of the estate as Miss Marion Borden died, and left most of the property to the Masonic Order. Due to the Great Depression, the estate was not settled in hopes that stocks and bonds would recover. The Masonic Order was forced to give up the estate due to financial reasons. It was purchased in 1943 by Dr. Cahen.

In 1951, the mansion was sold to J. Rowland Fitzgerald. The Bordens are buried in a private cemetery near the mansion.

Editor's note: Although the family and the Home Farm are legendary, there is little left of their legacy. The condensery is in ruins and most of the property has been carved up and sold. To preserve our rich heritage and history, we rely on Historic Societies and volunteer organizations like the Historical Society of Shawangunk and Gardiner who fight yearly to keep these places for future generations.

Bounty Cookbook

BORDEN'S MACARONI AND CHEESE
(courtesy the Historical Society of Shawangunk and Gardiner)

1/2 pound block of American Cheese (Borden called this "Chateau")
1 1/2 C. Scalded Milk
1/2 Tsp. Salt
2 fresh local eggs
1 C. cooked macaroni
2 Tbsp. Melted Butter
1/2 C. Bread Crumbs

Cut Chateau into small cubes. Scald milk in double boiler, add salt and Chateau. Stir until melted. Remove from fire and fold in slightly beaten eggs. Place cooked macaroni in a buttered baking dish, and pour melted cheese mixture over macaroni. Blend melted butter into bread crumbs and sprinkle on top of macaroni. Bake at 350 degrees for twenty minutes until crumbs are browned. Serves six.

BORDEN'S STUFFED CELERY
(courtesy the Historical Society of Shawangunk and Gardiner)

This recipe combines two of Orange County's finest products. Celery was a staple in the Black Dirt region for many years. Now onions have become the primary crop. Borden popularized American Cheese in the early 1900's. Neufchatel cheese; originating in Chester, can be substituted in this recipe; just omit the pimentos.

1/2 pound block of American Cheese (Borden calls this "Chateau")
2 Tbsps. Pimentos
8 Med. Stalks of Celery

Allow Chateau to stand at room temperature until soft. Then force through a sieve. Cut pimento finely and blend with cheese (can you tell this recipe comes from pre-food processor days?). Prepare celery and fill with cheese mixture. Chill and serve.

Eileen Piasecki-Couch is owner and CEO of the Pine Island Herb & Spice Co. Inc. She is a wife, a mother of three boys, a former research microbiologist, an accomplished pilot who flies regularly, and an artist. She has been painting for the last 7 years, and has recently started selling her work. www.pineislandherb.com.

GALEN'S SURPRISE MUFFINS
(courtesy of Liana Hoodes and Dave Church)

Dry Ingredients:
2 c. whole wheat pastry flour
3/4 c. unbleached white flour (or use all whole wheat pastry flour)
1 TB. baking powder
1/2 tsp. salt

Wet Ingredients:
2 fresh eggs
1/4 c. butter, melted (or light oil)
1/2 c. honey
1 c. milk
1 tsp. vanilla

3/4 c. each: fresh blueberries and cranberries. If you use frozen berries, do not defrost – mix straight from the freezer.

Preheat oven to 375. Grease muffin tins. Mix dries together. Mix wet together. If honey is hard, soften with butter/oil for 30 seconds in microwave, or in double boiler. Add Wet to Dry completely – don't over mix. Stir in berries gently and evenly. Fill greased muffin tins. Bake 35-40 minutes or until a toothpick stuck in comes out clean

Decadent Variation:
Instead of just berries, use 1/2 c. each: blueberries, cranberries, and chocolate chips. yeilds 12 servings.

"The first butter factory in America
was located in Campbell Hall."

Orange County Bounty Cookbook

Summer

(July, August September)

What's in season?

Fruits

- Apples (Mid July)
- Blueberries (Late July)
- Melons (August)
- Sweet Cherries (July)
- Tart Cherries (July)
- Peaches (late July)
- Pears (Mid August)
- Plums (September)
- Raspberries (July, Sept)

Vegetables

- Beans (July)
- Beets
- Broccoli
- Cabbage
- Carrots (late July)
- Cauliflower (Mid July)
- Celery (Mid July)
- Corn (Mid July)
- Cucumbers (Mid July)
- Eggplant (late July)
- Herbs (Cilantro, Parsley, Rosemary, Thyme)
- Lettuce (Mid May)
- Onions (July)
- Peas (until Aug)
- Peppers
- Potatoes (July)
- Radishes
- Spinach (August)
- Summer Squash
- Tomatoes (Mid July)
- Turnips (August)

Meats

- Chicken, Turkey, Pheasant
- Eggs

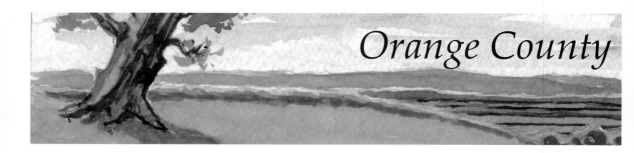

Shoprite
Florida, NY

Late in 1946, a sales representative from Del Monte Foods talked to several independent grocers around the area who all had the same problem – how to buy product cheaply enough to offer customers competitive prices. The representative introduced the grocers, who decided to try cooperative buying.

They experimented by ordering and splitting a few cases of grocery products. Pleased with the results, on December 5, 1946 they formalized the relationship. Each of the seven grocers invested $1,000 and Wakefern Food Corporation was born. The name came from the first letters of its founding members: W for Louis Weiss; A for Sam and Al Aidekman; K for Abe Kesselman; an E for pronunciation; and FERN for Dave Fern. Apparently they could not figure out a clever name to include a "G" for the other founders Sam Garb and Albert Goldberg!

From a small, struggling cooperative with seven members – all owners of their own grocery stores – ShopRite has grown into the largest retailer-owned cooperative in the United States. The cooperative is comprised of 43 members who individually own and operate supermarkets under the ShopRite banner. Today, more than 50,000 people are employed by Wakefern Food Corporation, the merchandising and distribution arm of the company, and the 190 ShopRite stores in New Jersey, New York, Connecticut, Pennsylvania and Delaware.

At ShopRite, generations of families have served generations of their customers' families. Although they have grown from small "Mom and Pop" stores of the 1940's, most of the ShopRite stores are still family owned and operated businesses – many with second, third, or even fourth generations involved.

Bounty Cookbook

SALSA
(courtesy of the Dolson Avenue, Middletown Produce Department)

2 cloves garlic
6-8 ripe local tomatoes
1 large local green pepper
1 large red pepper
1 local onions
2 poblano peppers
6 sprigs local cilantro
2 jalapeno peppers
salt
pepper

Dice up all ingredients and mix thoroughly. Refrigerate for 1 hour. Serve with tortilla chips or as a topping. Yields 6 servings.

"Good Pickin" by Janet Campbell

All ShopRite owners are members of Wakefern Food Corporation, which buys, warehouses and transports products while providing other support services to ensure customer satisfaction. "Volume" buying enables ShopRite stores to offer their consumers the lowest overall prices, and the greatest value, in the marketplace.

ShopRite now offers locally grown produce in many of its stores by purchasing directly from nearby farms. Look for signs in the produce section of your local ShopRite store. Look in the back of the book for a listing of Orange County ShopRite stores.

Janet Campbell has always had a love of art and nature. Her initial art education was in Botanical Illustration at the Bronx Botanical Garden. This led to an interest in watercolor and eventually an association with the Wallkill River School plein air painters. She serves as the Secretary of the Wurtsboro Art Alliance and her watercolors are exhibited in a variety of regional shows.

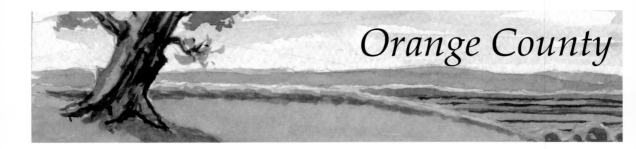

The Professional Image Marketing & Public Relations
Newburgh, NY

The Professional Image Marketing & Public Relations, a company founded in 1984, publishes several local magazines which have become valued resources in our community. This Newburgh-based publication group was founded by the husband and wife team of Terrie Goldstein and Clayton Buchanan.

Hudson Valley Parent magazine, first published in 1994, helps parents through that maze of parenthood. With

"New York Trilogy" by Clayton Buchanan.

its emphasis on finding the best local resources, the publication highlights local farms and farm markets together with special festivals that celebrate the heritage of the region.

For the older market, *Hudson Valley Life* features local restaurants, healthy eating tips and always seeks out unusual stories about local people and places.

Three years ago, Clayton, who studied in Provincetown Massachusetts, under noted expressionist painter Henry Hensche, returned to painting fulltime. His works have received accolades from our community. Locally he has been recognized for excellence by the *Kent Art Association,* the *Orange County Art Federation* and the *Washingtonville Art Society*.

Newburgh's East End historic district is home to more than 4000 historic buildings making it the largest in the state.."

Clayton Buchanan's paintings are in private and corporate collections in the U.S. and Canada; received Best in Show, 2006 Orange County Art Federation Member Exhibition; member Guild of Boston Artists, Boston, MA; resides and has studio in Newburgh, NY.

Bounty Cookbook

VEGETABLE STEW
(courtesy of Professional Image Marketing)

1/3 cup	extra virgin olive oil
3 cups	eggplant (2 small/ 1 large) cubed
2 cups	sweet potatoes (2-3) peeled and cubed
1 cup	portabella mushroom caps sliced
1 cup	potatoes (1) peeled and cubed
1 cup	tomatoes diced
1 cup	squash (1) peeled and cubed
1 cup	carrots peeled and diced
1/2 cup	scallions chopped • 1/2 cup onions diced
1/3 cup	fresh dill chopped • 1/3 cup fresh parsley chopped
6 cloves	garlic finely chopped or smashed
4 cups	veg. stock • 2 cups water • 1/3 cup chardonnay (optional)

AVOCADO CHILL

2	avocados, peeled and mashed
1 cup	sour cream
6 tbsp	fresh lemon juice
1/3 cup	fresh cilantro

In a bowl, mix avocado, sour cream, fresh lemon juice and cilantro until smooth (some chunks of avocado remaining in mix is fine). Cover and set in refrigerator to chill.

Make sure to have one large skillet and one large pot sitting on stove. In the skillet, heat 6 tbls olive oil, add garlic, and onions for about 2 minutes (barely soft), then add eggplant, and mushrooms. Cook for about 3-5 minutes on medium heat, stirring frequently. Using a spatula, remove vegetables and place the large pot. In the same skillet, heat 6 tbls olive oil from reserve, add sweet potatoes, and carrots. Cook for 3 minutes on medium heat until browned. Remove with spatula and add to large pot. In same skillet, heat remaining oil, add potatoes, scallions, and _ of the parsley,. Cook 5 minutes on medium heat until potatoes are slightly brown, add chardonnay wine and tomatoes , cook on high for 3 minutes. Remove from skillet with spatula and place in large pot. Add remaining parsley, fresh dill, vegetable stock, water and squash into large pot. Cook on med/low for 20-25 minutes. Let stand for 5 minutes, serve in bowl w/avocado chill. Yields 6 servings.

JADS Farm Market
PO Box 162
Pine Island, NY 10969

In a way, JADS Farm Market is named for the future.

It's an acronym of the first initials of the Madura children - Joshua, who's 8; Alyssa, 4; David, 2; and Skyler, 13. Kristie and John Madura named the market for the children, hoping that, in the future, they will carry on the mission.

"JADS Farm Market" by Karen Schoonmaker .

The Maduras opened the business in April 2007. Kristie says John wanted to grow local produce for local people.

The farm produces vegetables, spices, herbs, flowers, greens and more, all offered for sale at the market. "Bringing fresh food from my field to you," Kristie says, is the best part of the business.

When people eat local produce, she says, they're eating food that is fresher and healthier.

Pine Island's spring 2007 newsletter says that JADS occupies a prominent corner spot in Pine Island, where the Glowaczewski brothers ran a produce market for several years.

Madura, a veteran of New York City's green market economy, "heard the site was vacant and decided to gamble that people in the Pine Island region (would) support a local farm market," the newsletter said. Looks like the gamble is paying off.

Karen Schoonmaker - A landscape and still life painter, Karen divides her time between painting and teaching art in the Goshen, NY school district. Exhibiting locally and on Long Island, her work can be seen in print as well as in public and private collections.

Shawn Dell Joyce is a sustainable artist and activist, founder of the Wallkill River School, and writes a syndicated weekly column called "Sustainable Living" in the Sunday Times Herald Record. She has works in major museum collections, and private collections around the world. www.WallkillRiverSchool.com

Bounty Cookbook

FARM MARKET STYLE EGGPLANT
(courtesy of Kristie Madura)

2 LARGE WHITE/PURPLE EGGPLANT
2 LARGE RIPE TOMATOES
1 BUNCH BASIL
4 CLOVES GARLIC, MINCED
12 OZ. RICOTTA CHEESE
PARMESIAN CHEESE
12 OZ. FRESH MOZZARELLA
2 EGGS
2 TB. HEAVEY CREAM
2 C. ITALIAN STYLE BREAD CRUMBS
OLIVE OIL
4 C. FAVORITE MARINARA SAUCE

"Heirloom Eggplants" by Shawn Dell Joyce, (Pastel 2006)

PREHEAT OVEN TO 350 DEGREES

STRIPE EGGPLANT SKINS. SLICE DIAGONALLY INTO 1/4 INCH PIECES. SCRAMBLE EGGES AND HEAVEY CREAM TOGETHER. DIP EACH EGGPLANT SLICE INTO EGG MIXTURE, THEN COAT EACH SIDE WITH THE BREAD CRUMBS. DRIZZEL OIL OIL ON BAKING DISH, AND ARRANGE SLICES IN SINGLE LAYER. BAKE 15 MIN. EACH SIDE.

WHILE THIS IS BAKING: SLICE TOMATOES INTO 1/4 INCH PIECES, AND PULL 16-20 LEAVES FROM BASIL.

REMOVE BAKED EGGPLANT FROM OVEN AND LET DRAIN ON A PAPER TOWEL.

COVER THE BOTTOM OF A 9X11 BAKING DISH WITH 1 C. MARINARA. LINE BOTTOM OF DISH WITH EGGPLANT. TOP EACH PIECE WITH A SLICE OF TOMATO. SPRINKLE WITH 1/2 THE MINCED GARLIC. TOP THIS WITH 1/2 THE BASIL LEAVES. SCATTER SEVERAL SMALL TSP. OF RICOTTA THROUGH OUT DISH. SPRINKLE WITH MOZZARELLA. COVER WITH 2 C. MARINARA, AND REPEAT LAYERING.

COVER DISH WITH FOIL AND BAKE FOR 1 HR.

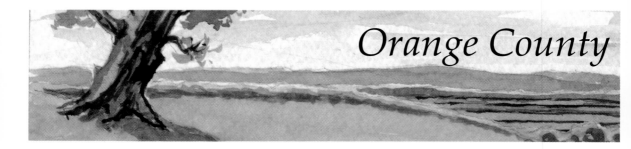

Sugar Loaf Mountain Herbs
1361 Kings Hwy., Ste C
Chester, NY 10918
(845) 469-6460

"Sugarloaf Mountain Herbs" by Shawn Dell Joyce

Even as a child, Alicia Frosini was interested in plants. By the time she was 12, she was earning wages by working with plants, and, even better, showing skill at it. She loved rescuing plants, bringing them back to life, and she was good at it.

After high school, Frosini went on to study horticulture formally. Later, she and her husband started a business, growing specialty plants and herbs. They've been growing the business for 25 years, and put down roots in Sugarloaf 13 years ago. Recently, they have expanded into retail, with a shop specializing in herbs, right in Sugarloaf.

In running her business, Frosini says, she is doing everything she loves. And, she says, she's meeting and spending time with people who share her love of herbs and of the Earth.

Eating locally makes sense on all sorts of levels, she believes. "I personally feel that if we want farmland in our region, we need to support our local farmers." And, she adds, it's a healthier approach to eating.

Frosini sees it happening. She sees people becoming more aware of their health, and of their own food habits. She sees increasing awareness of the global situation, and believes that supporting local business and supporting fair trade practices and businesses is helpful on a global level, too.

Working as a grower, retailing pots of herbs, "I'm constantly hearing how beautiful and healthy everything looks," she says. "Well, when things aren't being trucked hundreds of miles, it's common sense that you are getting a healthier plant, more reasonably prices. And that goes for local produce, as well."

Bounty Cookbook

PESTO
(courtesy of Sugar Loaf Mountain Herbs)

3 c. packed fresh basil leaves
3-4 cloves garlic
1/4 tsp. salt
3/4 c. parmesan cheese freshly grated
1/4c. pulverized nuts (pine, almonds or walnuts)
1/2c. olive oil
1/2c. fresh parsley
1/4c. melted better
pepper freshly ground

Puree everything together in a food processor filled with steel blade or use a mortar and pestle and coarse salt to pound the basil and garlic together. Stir in remaining ingredients. When using with pasta, use about 1 cup of pesto to 1 pound of pasta.

> *"Sugar Loaf, the craft hamlet, was named for the nearby mountain that is shaped the way sugar was formed and sold during Colonial days. The mountain has always had unusual interest and speculation surrounding it. Originally it was a Native American burial ground, and over the years various relics and bones have been uncovered here."*

Shawn Dell Joyce is a sustainable artist and activist, founder of the Wallkill River School, and writes a syndicated weekly column called "Sustainable Living" in the Sunday Times Herald Record. She has works in major museum collections, and private collections around the world. www.WallkillRiverSchool.com

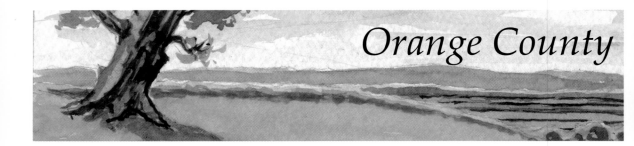

Angelo's Restaurant
4 North Main Street
Harriman, NY
(845) 781-4641

Darrel Lexandra is one of countless New Yorkers who rethought and rebuilt their lives after 9/11. For Lexandra, the change was a decision to spend more time with his family. And to open a restaurant.

Lexandra thought that Harriman would be a prefect place for a small, family-run restaurant. And, it turns out, it is. Lexandra owns and operates not one, but two, restaurants in Harriman.

The decision was a good one in emotional ways, too. Lexandra loves "knowing that the food we produce is the best we are able to do. Having guests of the restaurant compare our food, favorably, to their mother's and grandmother's home cooking."

"Angelos" by Bruce Thorne

Customers' comments echo Lexandra's: "Wonderful flavors, wonderful food, and it brings me back to my grandmother's kitchen each and every time I dine there. Makes you feel like you are in your own home," one wrote on a business website. "Heavenly!! A great place to savor a meal with friends and family," wrote another.

Lexandra values the connection he's built with customers, and the power of that connection within the larger realm of society. "Locally and privately owned restaurants," he says, "not the 'chains,' know their guests and are more concerned about our communities on all levels and should be supported by those in the communities.

"We are Harriman homeowners," he says. "Our kids were raised here and attended school here and we believe we have the greatest county to live and work in."

CHICKEN WITH TOMATOES AND CALAMATA OLIVES
(courtesy of the kitchen at Angelo's by Chef Carlo)

8 oz boneless Chicken Breast
1 cup bread crumbs
1/2 cup flour
1 eggs
2 lg fresh tomatoes
1/4 fresh basil
4 cloes garlic
1/2 cup red onion
12 pitted calamata olives
1/4 cup Feta cheese
pinch of salt
pinch of pepper
2 oz red vinegar
6 oz estra virgin olive oil
1/4 cup chopped parsley

"Rooster", by Lita Thorne

Pound chicken breast to 1/8inch thick. Flour, dip in egg (beaten) coat with bread crumbs. Saute cutlet in extra virgin olive oil, about 2 minutes on first side and 1 minute on other side. Remove from heat and set aside (keep warm). Saute garlic then add chopped tomatoes, olives, basil, red onion. Saute until tomatoes are cooked (about 3 minutes). Plate cutlet on top of tomatoes and olive mixture and top with crumbled feta cheese. Yield 1 servings

"The Lenape Nation that once occupied parts of
Orange County named the Kowawase Unique Area.
Kowawese (Kow-a-way-say) meant "place of small pines"
to the Lenape who once lived there."

Bruce Thorne-His style has been compared to Van Gogh for his rich color, thick impasto paint technique and his passion for painting.

Lita Thorne-Lita's grandparents' Blackfeet Indian heritage can be felt in her vibrant color palette and simple designs.

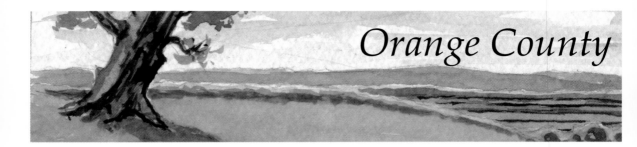

Acorn Hill
Farmstead Cheese
65 Red Barn Rd
Pine Bush, NY 12566
acornhill@hvc.rr.com

Joyce Henion of Acorn Hill
Farmstead Cheese of Pine Bush
said the business was born from
her desire to have fresh goat milk
and goat milk products for her
family. She started on her dream
and, in time,the business grew.
Acorn Hill joined the Pine Bush
Farmers' market as a vendor.
The goat herd grew, and the
business with it. Customers of the farmers'
market helped bring success.

"Acorn Hill" by Jacqueline Schwab.

Henion says that farming and cheese-making "allows me to share my love for healthy dairy
products made with the milk of animals that are managed holistically without hormones,
antibiotics, or chemical wormers."

Locally grown food, she says, is the freshest and most nutritious food possible. In addition,
the whole concept of eating locally helps support the economy and preserve open space.

"The Wallkill River
is the only river
in North America
that flows
North instead of South."

Bounty Cookbook

ROASTED FETA WITH OLIVE AND RED PEPPERS
(courtesy of Joyce Henion, Acorn Hill, Pine Bush)

1/2 lb. Feta cheese drained.
1/2 tsp. chopped oregano or marjoram
1/4 tsp. black pepper
1 large red pepper roasted and sliced
10 Kalmata olives pitted rinsed and chopped
2 TB. extra-virgin olive oil

"Playful Goats" by Jacqueline Schwal

Preheat broiler. Divide cheese evenly among 4 small baking dishes or in one larger dish. Sprinkle with oregano or marjoram and pepper. Stir together roasted red pepper, olives and oil in small bowl and spoon mixture over and around the feta cheese. Broil 2 to 4 inches from flame until edges of the cheese turn golden, about 5 minutes.
  Yield 4 servings

"Kurt Seligmann, a famous American surrealist painter
lived with his wife Arlette in Sugar Loaf.
The couple helped many German and Jewish
intellectuals escape Nazi persecution during the war.
Their home was donated
to the Orange County Citizens Foundation
who preserve its artistic legacy."

Jacqueline Schwab is an oil painter living in Pine Bush, New York. She paints with the Wallkill River School. She studied painting at SUNY at New Paltz and the Woodstock School of Art

Royal Acres Farm
Scotchtown Collabar Road
Middletown, NY
(845) 692-6719

"Royal Acres" by Carrie Jacobson

John King, of Royal Acres Farm in Middletown, says he's always been around farms. When he was growing up, his family had a farm upstate, outside Oneonta. His uncle had a farm in Virginia. King had farming in his bones.

The joy of it, for him, is that "it's the type of business that you can see." You plant, you water, you tend, and it grows. Yes, there's weather and there are animals, but that's part of it. King enjoys working outside, and, he says, when you're a farmer, you're your own boss. It helps that he's got three great kids who are willing to shoulder some of the responsibility.

The trend toward eating locally is important, King believes, though he muses about what people are willing to pay. Locally grown food might cost less, but then again, it might not. Quality and freshness don't come cheap. Many of the farmers King knows, good farmers, too, work full-time jobs in addition to farming. It's a sweet life, but not an easy one.

"If you support local farmers," King says, "local farmers will stay in business. A lot of people think farming is a hobby. It's not. It's a business."

Farms, he says, stimulate the economy in all sorts of ways. The money that people spend locally tends to stay local. Farmers buy seed and supplies and machinery and tools and equipment from local sellers. They, in turn, employ local people, and buy what they can locally. The money stays in the community, and everyone benefits.

King raises his crop in two spots, at Royal Acres on the Scotchtown Collabar Road in Middletown, and on 10 Black Dirt acres. He concentrates the root vegetables in Pine Island, and grows some of the same crops at each place, so there will be a good and timely supply. He and his family start all the plants at Royal Acres. They bring their fruit and produce, their

ZUCCHINI PIE
(recipes courtesy of John King's mother)

3 c. diced or grated zucchini (wash zucchini first; do not peel. Cut in half and remove seeds before dicing or grating)
1 large onion, diced or grated
1/2 c. grated parmesan and 1/2 c. grated cheddar
1/2 c. salad oil
1 c. Bisquick
4 eggs
3-4 TB minced parsley • salt and pepper

Combine all ingredients until zucchini is nicely coated. Pour into greased pan - 9-inch by 9-inch, or two 9-inch pie pans or three 7-inch round pans. Bake at 375 degrees for 35-40 minutes, or until lightly browned.

ZUCCHINI BREAD
2 c. shredded raw zucchini • 2 c. sugar • 1 c. cooking oil
3 eggs • 1 tsp. vanilla • 3 c. flour
1/4 tsp. baking soda • 1/2 tsp. salt • 1 tsp. ginger
1/2 tsp. cloves • 1 c.. chopped nuts

optional: 1/2 c. raisins or 1/2 c. chocolate chips

Combine sugar (use a little less if you're including raisins and chocolate chips), oil, eggs, vanilla. Stir in zucchini. Mix dry ingredients and blend into mixture. Add nuts and optional raisins and chocolate chips. Pour into greased loaf pans. Bake at 325 degrees for an hour or until done.

---

annuals, perennials and herbs to the markets in Newburgh and Pine Bush.

The recipes that King shared are from his mother's kitchen.

Carrie Jacobson came to painting when she was 50; she felt it was her soul singing out. People enjoy her landscapes and her paintings of dogs and cats, her favorite subjects.

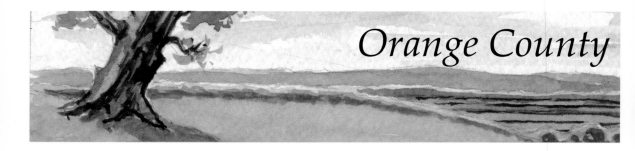

Wildfire Grill

74 Clinton Street
Montgomery, NY 12549
www.wildfire-grill.com
(845) 457-3770

Krista Wild began the Wildfire Grill about six years ago. The restaurant grew out of her enjoyment of cooking and entertaining.

The best part of the business for Wild, who is the chef as well as the owner, is being creative with different products through the different seasons,

"Wildfire Grill" by Marge Morales.

creating and perfecting dishes that make the most of fresh vegetables or fruit, and which showcase local produce in tasty and appealing ways.

Supporting the local economy by eating locally, and using local produce in the restaurant is a way to help the community itself grow and prosper, Wild says.

She adds that she'd like her neighbors to know that at the Wildfire Grill, "we use the freshest products available. Everything is made here in house, including all of our desserts."

"Kate Seraday, a fine artist and children's book illustrator who was a contemporary of Beatrix Potter lived and worked on Kaisertown Road in Montgomery."

Bounty Cookbook

PEACH COBBLER
(courtesy of Wildfire Gril)

Ingredients:
6 large, ripe peaches, peeled, pitted and cut into
1/4 inch slices (about 4 cups)
3 tablespoons flour
5 tablespoons sugar

Pastry topping:
3 cups all purpose flour
1/2 teaspoon salt
4 tablespoons firmly packed brown sugar
2 teaspoons baking powder
3/4 stick cubed butter
3/4 cup heavy cream

"Peaches" by Lisa O'Gorman-Hofsommer.

Instructions:
Preheat over to 350 degrees

In small bowl, combine peaches sugar and flour. Toss gently to coat. Place into an 8-inch pie dish.

In a large mixing bowl combine flour, salt, brown sugar and baking powder. Work the butter in with your hands until it becomes crumbly. Then top the peaches with the crumb mix and bake.

Bake about 40 minutes or until golden brown. Served topped with vanilla ice cream and fresh whipped cream. Yield 4 servings

Marge Morales of Rock Tavern sees herself as a modern-day storyteller, using paint as her medium. In oils and watercolors, Marge offers more than images; her art tells stories that touch the heart and the soul.

Lisa O'Gorman-Hofsommer, born & raised in Yonkers, N.Y., moved to the Hudson Valley in 1990. Has been painting in pastels since then. She has a strong desire to paint wildlife & landscapes. Created a Pet Portraits business. Petportraitsnmore.com. Been painting with the Wallkill River School for four years.

Ochs Orchard
4 Ochs Lane
Warwick, NY
(845) 986-1591

"Ochs Orchard" by Eileen Piasecki-Couch

Susan Ochs is living her dream, and keeping her father's dream alive, too.

Susan and her son, Allen, are the third generation of Ochses to run Ochs Orchard in Warwick. In the late 1930s, it was owned and managed through the partnership of Peter Ochs and Chris Scheuermann. They ran the wholesale apple and peach fruit farm until 1969, when Ochs bought out his partner.

In 1971, Peter's son, Leslie, began to operate the orchard. In 1973, Leslie and his wife Susan bought the farm from Peter and began promoting the retail trade by opening a farm stand. Wanting to diversify, to offer more to their customers, they began growing vegetables.

They started a pick-your-own apples business, which became very successful. Eventually, the cider press was installed and fresh cider was made every week.

These days, the farm is run by Susan and her son, Allen. Allen has grown the farm to include a wide variety of fresh fruit, like nectarines, raspberries, blackberries, apricots, plums, pears, peaches and more than a dozen varities of apples, many of which are pick-your-own. You can also pick your own flowers from thier extensive flower garden.

Susan says, "Being a farmer brings me back to my roots. My dad was a farmer, and he devoted his life to the orchard. I feel like I am sharing his dream."

Susan says she and Allen are dedicated to providing the best possible produce for their customers. And their customers' satisfaction is tops with them.

Eating locally is good for the farms, the neighbors and the community, Susan believes.

"Best of all," she says, "you know where your food comes from. If you have a question about your food, you just ask the farmer."

Bounty Cookbook

OCHS WALDORF SALAD
(courtesy of Susan Ochs)

1 red delicious apple
1 stalk celery
1/4 c. walnut pieces
1/4 c. NY state cheddar cheese
3 TB. mayonnaise
Optional additions: 1/4 c. chicken,
1/4 c. raisins, 1/4 c. hard cooked eggs
or 1/4 c. flaked tuna

"Ochs Dairy Farm" by John Creagh

Quarter apple but do not peel. Cut out core and cube. Cut celery into small pieces. Cube cheese. Mix all ingredients together, adding more mayonnaise, if desired. Serve over a bed of lettuce, or mixed greens. Yield 2 servings

*"The Hudson River was originally called Mahicanituk
by the Native Americans living on its shores.
It meant "continually flowing water."
In 1609 with hopes of finding a northeast passage,
Henry Hudson sailed his ship the Half Moon
up the river that now bears his name.."*

Eileen Piasecki-Couch is owner and CEO of the Pine Island Herb & Spice Co. Inc. She is a wife, a mother of three boys, a former research microbiologist, an accomplished pilot who flies regularly, and an artist. She has been painting for the last 7 years, and has recently started selling her work. www.pineislandherb.com.

John Creagh has been a painter and an instructor for over 25 years, as well as a member and instructor for the Wallkill River School. His artwork is featured in many private collections around the world, you can visit him at www.jcreagh.com

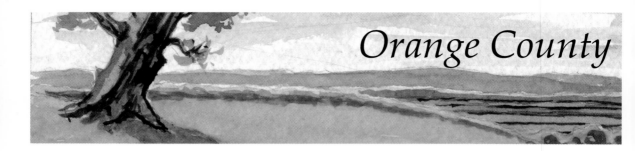

Hoeffner Farm
405 Goodwill Rd
Montgomery, NY 12549
(845) 457-3453

It was roughly 1918 when the Hoeffner family left Hicksville, on Long Island, to come to Orange County. Land near Hicksville was growing increasingly expensive, taxes were rising, and it was time to find greener pastures, literally and figuratively.

"Hoeffner's Farm" Pastel by Shawn Dell Joyce.

The family found a home in Montgomery, and in 2005, celebrated 80 years on their farm. In 2006, the farm was mentioned in a "New York" magazine article on New York City's Union Square Greenmarket - the Hoeffners have brought produce to the market for 30 years.

Hoeffner Farm grows a variety of vegetable and bedding plants. It offers hanging baskets, fruits and vegetables in season, U-pick pumpkins, hayrides and Christmas trees.

The Hoeffners say their favorite part of the work is being outside, watching the plants grow, and then enjoying the warmth of the greenhouses in the winter.

That people across the country and across the region are seeing the value of eating locally is, of course, a great benefit. "Finally!" a Hoeffner farmer says.

The freshness of the produce is only part of the appeal of eating food grown close to home, they say. The fruits and vegetable are "cleaner, healthier - picked at the peak of growth." It's a change for the better.

The roadside stand, the Hoeffners say, is great for meeting people and making them aware of all the different foods available in the area.

There's promise for the future, they say. Younger people are realizing that " locally grown is healthier, more nutritious and, the best part is that it tastes so much better."

Bounty Cookbook

FRESH FRUIT PIE
(courtesy of Hoeffner Farms)

"Hoeffner's Fields" Pastel by Shawn Dell Joyce.

PIE CRUST
1-1/2 c. all-purpose flour
1/2tsp. salt
1 TB. sugar

CUT IN WITH PASTRY BLENDER:
1/2c. shortening – Crisco
1/3 c. or 5 TB. tap water
Mix together – divide in half – roll out

FILLING
1 c. sugar
1/2c. all-purpose flour
1/4tsp. salt
3/4tsp. nutmeg

Mix sugar, flour and salt. Sprinkle a small amount in pastry lined pan. Combine fruit and mix. Put in pie shell, dot with butter – cut up 2 TB. put on top crust, cut a few slits for steam to escape. Bake in a preheated hot oven 425 degrees for 40-50 minutes. Let cool and Top with whipped cream, ice cream or frozen custard. Yield 6-8 servings

Fruit for pie can be substituted according to season:
Fresh rhubarb – 4 c.
Rhubarb and strawberries – 2 c. each
Strawberries and blueberries – 2 c. each
Blueberries and peaches – 2 c. each

Shawn Dell Joyce is a sustainable artist and activist, founder of the Wallkill River School, and writes a syndicated weekly column called "Sustainable Living" in the Sunday Times Herald Record. She has works in major museum collections, and private collections around the world. www.WallkillRiverSchool.com

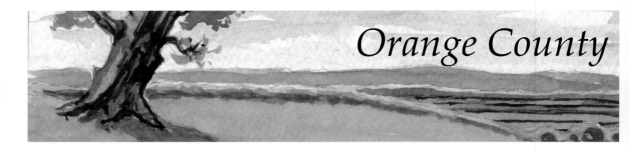
Warwick Valley Winery
114 Little York Road
Warwick, NY 10990
(845) 258-6020
http://www.wvwinery.com

"Warwick Valley Winery" by
Gloria Detore Mackie

Warwick Valley Winery had its start in 1989, when Joseph
Grizzanti, Jason Grizzanti and Jeremy Kidde bought the orchard
began learning how to cultivate fruit. Local apple growers and
extension agents taught them the basics, and helped them sip
early success.

The winery's first product - its entire business, really - came as
the result of an apple crop so abundant that that the new owners
had enough produce to start an experiment: They tried making
hard cider.

The experiment worked. The owners were hooked, and the winery opened in the fall
of 1994.

Warwick Vallery Winery believes its success has its roots in the owners' insistence on using
the finest available fruit in their beverages.

"Our mission since our inception has been to create fruit-based alcoholic beverages that are
as unique as the fruits themselves," theysay.

The Grizzantis and Kidde believe that the best communities are sustainable. Food that
comes from local farmers, grown in local fields, cooked and eaten by local people forms a
healthy and strong community. Society, they believe, is too often detached from this model.
They're happy to see the trend turning back to what they call a "simple, yet progressive way
of life."

WHITE WINE SANGRIA KIR
(courtesy of Warwick Valley Wine Co., Inc.)

750ml. bottle Warwick Valley Winery
        Harvest Moon
1 c. (8 oz) American Fruits Black Currant
        Liqueur
1-2 lemons, cut in 1/2-inch slices
1-2 oranges, cut in 1/2-inch slices
1 c. black currants (or substitute with
        blackberries, black raspberries)
Club soda (1 oz per 6 oz sangria)
Fresh mint sprigs

In a large pitcher, combine the Harvest Moon,
black currant liqueur, lemons, oranges and
black currants, stir gently. Garnish with
fresh mint. Refrigerate several hours, but
preferably overnight, to allow the flavors to
develop. Top with club soda if desired.
Serves 6.

"Grapes" by M.E.Whitehill

"The mineral Warwickite can be found

only in the town it is named for

and no where else in the world!"

Gloria Detore Mackie is a licensed social worker who practices in Goshen.She is the creator of "Art for Earth;" a nonprofit cultural consciousness-raising event series combining dance, visual arts and environmental speakers.

Mary Evelyn Whitehill has over 27 years of watercolor experience and is a demonstrating artist for the Wallkill River School. She is also the great-granddaughter of Hudson River School artist Thomas Pope. www.mewhitehill.com

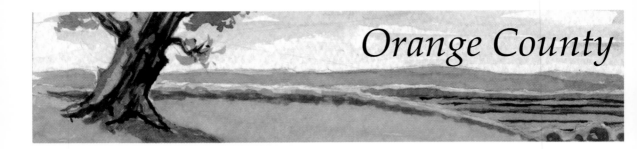

Overlook Farm Market and Country Store

5417 Route 9W
Newburgh, NY 12550
(845) 562-5780
www.overlookfarmmarket.com

Overlook Farm Market came into being 25 years ago, when Jim "the farmer," and Nina "the market touch," joined forces. At that time, there were plenty of farms, but very few direct markets. Jim and Nina saw that customers needed access to the produce, and Overlook was born.

These days, they find a generation that understands and appreciates the value of farm-fresh produce. Nina says she and Jim appreciate the opportunity to present themselves and the farm market as stewards of our land, and love showing their commitment to the community they serve.

"Minding the Farm", by Pat Morgan.

They value the chance to "strip away the layers of corporate waste, simplify and return to basic rituals." Health, good will, individual expression and respect for the land and the community form the backbone of their effort.

The Overlook Farm Market and Country Store has offered produce and more on Route 9W for many generations. In addition to the local fruits and vegetables, Overlook offers a petting zoo, a bakery, a deli and a garden center.

"Our market and farm has been here for many generations," Nina says, "and with the awareness currently about our value and service will continue from March until January for many years to come."

Bounty Cookbook

CORN SOUFFLE
(courtesy of Overlook Farm)

16 oz. of fresh corn (or frozen)
1 c. milk
3 eggs
2 TB. sugar
salt and pepper to taste
1 TB. butter, cut into 6 pieces

Pour all ingredients into a blender. Blend on medium until mixed thoroughly. Pour into a medium sized baking dish coated with cooking spray. Dot the top with butter pieces. Bake at 325 degrees for 1 hour 10 minutes. Yield 6-8 servings.

FARMERS' MARKET COUSCOUS
(courtesy of Overlook Farm)

2 c. water
2 garlic cloves, chopped
1 TB. olive oil
1 c. uncooked couscous
1 c. diced zucchini
2 c. chopped greens
1/2 c. crumbled feta cheese
1/4 c. chopped fresh basil
1/2 tsp. salt

Bring water to a boil over medium heat in a 6-cup saucepan. Add garlic and olive oil. Stir in couscous, zucchini and greens. Remove from heat. Cover and allow to stand 10 minutes. Add feta, basil and salt; toss gently. Yield 4 servings.

Pat Morgan, a watercolor painter, has studied with artists including Richard Ochs, Eli Rosenthal and Mel Stabin. Currently, she is represented by the Wallkill River Gallery. She has received local and regional awards for her work, and enjoys teaching other painters her love of watercolor.

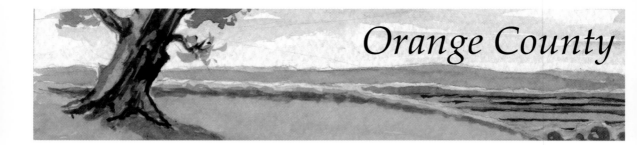

La Vera Cucina
43 Hillside Terrace
Monroe, NY 10950
845-774-3340
www.laveracucina.net

Alex Raja and his brother Tony started La Vera
Cucina 10 years ago in Suffern, later moving to
their current home in Monroe. The brothers love
to cook the Italian cuisine they grew up with.
They say they also enjoy sharing the happiness
of their satisfied customers.

"La Vera Cucina" Pastel by Mary Sealfon.

 Both brothers, Tony says, believe in supporting the community. The restaurant is full of
paintings bought from local artists, and Tony travels to Hunts Point twice a week for meat
and fish. He loves to use fresh local herbs and produce in the summer.

"You can get the best in Orange County," he says, "without traveling far."

"Beets" by Alix Travis.

Bounty Cookbook

SALMON LA VERA CUCINA
(courtesy of La Vera Cucina)

1 filet salmon
1/3 cup olive oil
1/2 cup balsamic vinegar
4 garlic cloves (keep whole)
fresh rosemary (several sprigs worth)
fresh basil (a handful of leaves torn or chopped)
flour
salt
pepper
1 Tbls butter
Portobello mushroom, spinach and lemon

Dust salmon on flour sprinkle filet with salt and pepper. Saute filet in pan over med-high heat. After several minutes add whole garlic cloves. Turn salmon after 4 minutes (or fewer if you like it rare). Add rosemary and basil. Saute 2 more minutes then add balsamic vinegar. Cook down for a minute, add butter.

Serve over a grilled portabello (you can also saute the portabello if you don't have a grill) and sauted spinach in garlic, lemon and oil. Yield 2 servings

"Monroe is the birthplace of Velveeta Cheese."

Mary Mugele Sealfon received a BA in painting at the U of California at Santa Barbara and a MA from NYU. In New York City she pursued a career as an Art Director and designer. She has won numerous awards and her paintings and prints have been exhibited nationally and internationally. She also teaches art locally, including SUNY Orange.

Alix Hallman-Travis is an award-winning watercolorist who believes in painting every day, from life, and all at once. She is a demonstrating artist for the Wallkill River School, and is represented by several galleries including the Wallkill River Gallery.

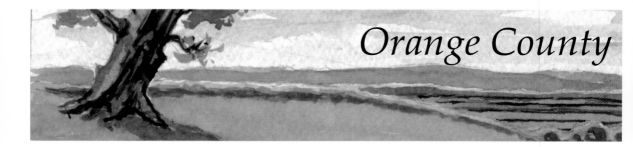

Port Java Cafe
19 Front St
Port Jervis, NY 12771
(845) 858-4500

Judy Rudy opened Port Java in 2005, after her job as human resources director was absorbed by the company. She'd always wanted to do coffee and books, she says. Her husband put it to her. Now or when?

Rudy said "Now.."

"Port Java Cafe" by Carrie Jacobson.

Port Java is a sanctuary in the heart of Port Jervis. Comfortable chairs and couches encourage relaxation. Wireless connections allow folks to work, write, surf, whatever, while spending time in the cafe, or sitting at its sidewalk tables. Friday and Saturday nights, there's live entertainment. And always, there's a warm welcome, a cup of coffee or tea, art on the walls, and a fine, easy menu - including great desserts.

The cafe, at 19 Front St., at the edge of the railroad tracks, reflects the railroad history of the town. From the charming logo, to the name, to the collection of historic photos, the theme of Port and the railroads lives in the cafe.

Judy's glad to see the trend toward home-grown eating. She began buying locally, at the Port Jervis Farmers' Market, and from farms in the area, before the idea grew on a grass-roots level. It just made sense to her, she says, and is happy that families and restaurants around the region are jumping on the bandwagon.

In a world that can be too hectic, and a town that can be too busy, Port Java is a great place to meet friends, to have a quiet cup of coffee, to relax and watch the world go on its way.

Here's Judy Rudy's recipe for a garden-filled flat bread sandwich, offered with seasonal vegetables.

Bounty Cookbook

FLAT BREAD SANDWICH
(courtesy of Port Java Cafe)

2 tomatoes
4 small zucchinis, yellow squash or a mix
2 regular and/or hot yellow peppers
2 red or white onions
1/2 lb. mushrooms
Spinach, when in season
1 wheel of brie
4 flat breads, cut in half

Cut the brie into slices. Cut veggies in thick slices and grill all, except for spinach

Pile on four halves of the flat bread

Top with brie and spinach and, if you like, a little olive oil. Press in panini pan, or any sort of contact grill (or in a skillet), until the flat bread is toasty and the brie runny. Yield 6 servings

"Port Jervis was the first stop on the "Old Mine Road" known as the first 100 mile road in America. The road was built by Dutch settlers who sought mines of gold and copper along the Delaware River Highlands."

Carrie Jacobson came to painting when she was 50; she felt it was her soul singing out. People enjoy her landscapes and her paintings of dogs and cats, her favorite subjects.

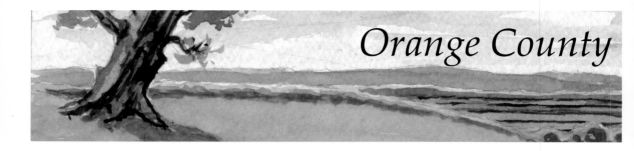

La Petite Cuisine
20 Railroad Ave.
Warwick, NY 10990
(845) 988-0988

"Mixed Vegtables" by Rosalind Hodgkins.

La Petite Cuisine, a Paris-feel cafe on the streets of Warwick, is owned and run by Patty Flynn. It features delicious traditional cafe breakfasts and lunches, including breads, baked goods and cheeses, sandwiches and salads, soups, crepes and desserts. Whenever possible, Flynn and her staff use locally grown produce, often from the War-wick farmers' market.

Chef Donna Hirsch, one of Flynn's staffers, is a self-taught chef on a three-decade apprenticeship. After being trained as a vegetarian chef on Cape Cod, she came to work in Warwick, and decided to live in town.

Hirsch became a chef because, she says, "I always had a knack for cooking and I was afraid I wouldn't make any money as an artist."

She's been predominantly interested in health and healthy foods - and in offering fresh, tasty, healthy alternatives. "I seem to run into lots of people with dietary issues," she says, "and I seem to always be able to say, 'Look what you can eat!' when they're at their wits' end with all of their restrictions."

Hirsch says her neighbors and friends already know a lot about her. "I am a pretty open book," she says, "...Someday I hope to add 'collage artist' to my vocational history."

"One of the great Hudson River painters,
Jasper Cropsey, moved to Warwick in 1869
and built a 29-room mansion and studio
that he named "Aladdin."

Bounty Cookbook

CHILLED CUCUMBER-YOGURT SOUP
(courtesy of Donna Kaminski)

6 large cucumbers
2 large cloves of garlic
2 - 32oz. containers of a plain yogurt
1 lemon
3 tablespoons honey or maple syrup (optional)
fresh dill - about 1/4 cup chopped or 2 tablespoons dried
2 teaspoons cracked pepper (or large grain black pepper)
1 teaspoon sea salt

Peel and quarter cucumbers, take out seeds. Grate one cucumber and set aside. In blender or food processor: puree cucumbers with yogurt in batches, if neccessary, adding garlic through a garlic press directly into mixture. Once pureed, put into large mixing bowl.

Add to mixture the honey or maple syrup, chopped or dried dill, pepper and salt. Squeeze the lemon through a strainer omitting seeds and add to mixture. Add grated cucumber and stir to thoroughly combine.

Set aside in refrigerator for at least one hour or more to thoroughly chill before serving. As this soup gets better after a day, stored in an air tight container, it can be eaten over a few days or prepared for a party a day or two ahead of time. You can top it with a sprig of dill when serving or a thin slice of lemon.
  Yield 8 servings

This is one of the recipes I brought to the cafe'. It hails from my health food days - I made this regularly for a client of mine and thought it would be a nice addition to our summer menu. This recipe makes enough for a party as it can serve at least 12. It has become very popular - it is refreshing , nourishing and light on a hot day._You can easily double this recipe with a consistent result. You can omit the honey or maple syrup, but I think adding a touch of sweetness increases the depth of flavor.

Rosalind Hodgkins recently moved to Orange County from NYC, she graduated from Pratt Institute and had an art career in NYC for 40 years. She has exhibited her work in United States, Canada & England. Since moving here her interest has been botanicals, landscapes and still lifes using watercolor painting medium that focuses on detail and the luminosity of color.

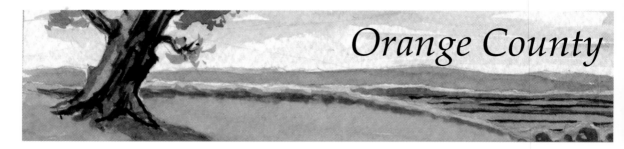

Ward's Bridge Inn
(formerly C.B. Driscoll's)
135 Ward St
Montgomery, NY 12549
(845) 457-1300
www.wardsbridgeinn.com

In 2005, Brian Pskowski saw an opportunity to bring the past to life. There was a tradition, and a name, and an idea that he could revive, he says. And an atmosphere he knew he could create, a comfortable spot where people could gather for a good meal. This, Pskowski says, is the Wards Bridge Inn.

The inn takes its name from the bridge that crosses the Wallkill River

In 2007, Pskowsk finds that he treasures "the freedom of creativity I have." He gets great satisfaction from creating and designing dishes and using "the freshest and finest ingredients available to me, especially locally grown."

"Ward's Bridge Inn" by Shawn Dell Joyce.

People who eat food grown close to home, and restaurateurs who use locally grown and locally raised produce in their menus enjoy fresh taste and quality. It's a decision, too, Pskowski says, that helps support the local farm industry.

"I am a local person who enjoys people, and enjoys feeding them our creative menu (sic) in addition to traditional dishes, great wine list, and family warmth, make for a relaxing and satisfying visit."

This is another spot that has changed hands a number of times in recent years, but it took Brian Pskowski and his team to create the perfect restaurant for this space. Neither too formal nor too casual, the food, service and ambiance strike the perfect balance to fulfill the promise of this terrific old building.

Bounty Cookbook

SCALLOPS AND SWEET CORN
(courtesy of Brian Pskowski, Chef, Ward's Bridge Inn)

2 cups cooked Arborio rice
16 sea scallops
2 ears of fresh local corn
3 shallots
1 bunch fresh parsley from the farmer's market
12 grape tomatoes from the farmer's market
1 cup white wine
salt and pepper to taste

Pan sear the scallops and set aside. Cut off the corn from the cob, and sweat until tender, then puree half.

Mince the shallots and add to the pan after the scallops. Deglaze with white wine. Chop the fresh parsley and add to taste.

Cut the fresh grape tomatoes in half, and combine with the rest of the ingredients. Serve immediately. Yield 6 servings

" In 1881, John Gail Borden,
heir to the Borden Condensed Milk Company,
started a self-sufficient utopian community
on a 2,000 acre farm in Montgomery.
It was developed as a place where
beauty and respect for nature
were as important as functional productivity.."

Shawn Dell Joyce is a sustainable artist and activist, founder of the Wallkill River School, and writes a syndicated weekly column called "Sustainable Living" in the Sunday Times Herald Record. She has works in major museum collections, and private collections around the world. www.WallkillRiverSchool.com

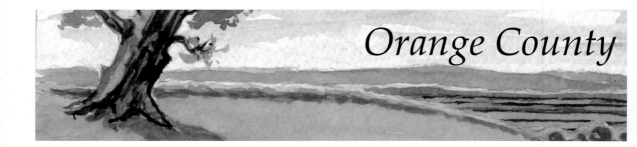

Restaurant 20 Front
20 Front St., Port Jervis
845-856-8955
www.twentyfront.com

Daniel J. Weber, the executive chef of 20 Front, graduated from the Pennsylvania Institute of Culinary Arts in 1998. After an apprenticeship at Skytop Lodge in the Poconos, he eventually became executive sous chef, responsible for all of the resort's food establishments.

At Skytop, Weber met Troy Chmielewski, a 2002 CIA graduate. The two became friends, and when Weber and his cousin, Michael Ely, began the restaurant, Chmielewski joined as an assistant chef.

"20 Front" by Carrie Jacobson

Restaurant 20 Front fills a lovely, historic building in downtown Port Jervis. The National Bank and Trust of Port Jervis built the structure as its headquarters, in 1914. In time, the bank took over the adjacent building; that's the structure that houses the restaurant today.

The high ceilings, marble columns, marble floor and architectural embellishments, inside and out, communicate presence, standing and a rich sense of history. The restaurant even uses the bank's two vaults, one as temporary storage, the other as a wine cellar.

Weber says he's proud of 20 Front's three culinary-school-trained chefs, and of the food and service the restaurant provides. "The whole staff goes above and beyond," he says. "We want the restaurant to be a dining experience."

Bounty Cookbook

SCALLOPS 20 FRONT
(courtesy of Chef Troy Chmielewski, Restaurant 20 Front)

2 oz. whole butter • 4 jumbo sea scallops • 1 chorizo sausage, sliced
1 qt. chicken stock • 1 oz. shallots, minced • 1/2 oz. garlic, minced
4 baby yellow beets • 4 baby red beets
1 Yukon Gold potato, medium dice • 4 oz. carrots, medium dice
1 cup flagolet beans, soaked overnight • 4 oz. fennel, sliced thin (reserve fronds for garnish) • 4 oz. green beans (haricots verts)
4 asparagus spears • 1/2 cup sherry, (Not grocery-store sherry)
1 oz. coriander, ground • 1 oz. basil, chiffonaded (chopped into strips)
1 oz. parsley, minced • salt and pepper to taste

Bring two pots of water to a boil and cook the yellow and red beets separately until tender, about 6 minutes. Remove from pot and shock in icewater. (Shocking stops the cooking process and maintains color.)

Bring two more large pots to a boil and cook the carrots and potatoes separately until tender. Remove from pot and shock. After the potatoes and carrots are cooked, quickly blanch the haricots verts and asparagus for 1-2 minutes, then shock in ice-water.

Heat the saucepan first, then add the butter and the scallops (doing it this way keeps the scallops from sticking). Sea, cooking until one side is caramel-colored. Remove scallops, and into the same pan, add the fennel and chorizo. Reduce the flame to low heat and saute for 5 minutes. Add the shallots and garlic; cook 1 minute more.

Deglaze the pan with sherry, add the chicken stock, coriander and beans, simmer until beans are tender, 10-12 minutes. Allow the broth to simmer for an additional 7-10 minutes.

Combine the rest of the blanched vegetables and scallops. On a low simmer, cook until the scallops are at medium doneness (3-4 minutes). Garnish with the fennel fronds and herbs. Season with salt and pepper to taste. Yield 4 servings

Carrie Jacobson came to painting when she was 50; she felt it was her soul singing out. People enjoy her landscapes and her paintings of dogs and cats, her favorite subjects.

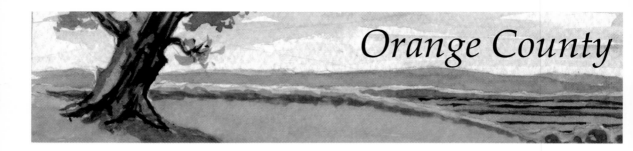

Hudson Valley Coffee Roasters
639 Broadway
Newburgh, NY 12550
(845) 561-6860
www.hudsonvalleyroasters.com

When Nicolo Zarcone started high school, he says, "I also entered the work force - I held a full-time job in a pizzeria. When I graduated from high school, I left for the adventures of the high seas."

"Hudson Valley Roasters" by Ellen Trayer

He became a boatswain's mate in the U.S. Navy, had as much adventure as anyone could want, and became friends with one of the ship's cooks. That friend talked Zarcone into taking a cooking course while the ship was in drydock.

Zarcone went for fun, and found his calling. "I felt fulfilled," he says.

After the Navy, he went to culinary school. From there, he went on to restaurant management school, where the fascination with coffee began.

Angela Monteleone, who had established herself in Newburgh as a banker, joined Zarcone - first as a behind-the-scenes partner in Hudson Valley Coffee Roasters, and then as an active partner. As the website implies, Monteleone went from bean-counter to (coffee) bean counter.

Hudson Valley Coffee Roasters started with a tiny storefront and a coffee roaster that, according to the website, was "worth more than Nick's car." It soon outgrew the spot, and found its home in an old factory building on a wide, sunny stretch of Broadway.

"Every morning when I walk into my place," Zarcone says, "I feel like I just stepped into a loft in SoHo."

In his menu, Zarcone uses lots of local ingredients, some of which he grows himself. "You should see my garden," he says. "It has everything. Today, my customers will eat vine ripened tomatoes with fresh mozzarella and string beans from my garden."

Bounty Cookbook

PENNE PASTA PRIMAVERA WITH GOAT CHEESE SAUCE
(courtesy of Nick Zarcone, Hudson Valley Coffee Roasters)

1/2 c. broccoli florets
1/2 c. asparagus tips
1/2 c. onion, diced
1/3 c. yellow or red bell peppers, diced
1 TB. garlic, minced
3/4 c. cherry tomato, halved
1/4 c. frozen peas
1 TB fresh parsley, chopped
3-1/2 oz. goat cheese, crumbled
parmesan cheese
penne pasta

Bring a large pot of salted water to a boil for the penne. Sweat the broccoli, asparagus, onion and bell pepper in 1 tablespoon of oil in a large nonstick skillet over medium heat. Cook until onion begins to turn translucent, about 5 minutes; then add the garlic, sauté one minute more. Meanwhile cook pasta in boiling water. Add a ladle of the pasta water to the pan with the vegetables. Simmer until the vegetables are crisp-tender, about 3 more minutes. Stir in crumbled goat cheese. Add tomatoes, peas and parsley. Transfer the pasta from the water to the pan with the vegetables using tongs to toss and coat with the sauce. Cook on low heat a couple of minutes. Divide among four plates and top with parmesan cheese. Yield 4 servings

---

Local producers, local farms, local growers, Zarcone believes, have a superior product that can never be duplicated by the mass producers.

"Buy local foods," he says. "Do it for your health!"

Ellen Trayer started painting in her thirties. Retiring to the Hudson Valley she became a member of the Wallkill River School studying under Shawn Dell Joyce and Gene Bove. Contact information eltray@msn.com,

---

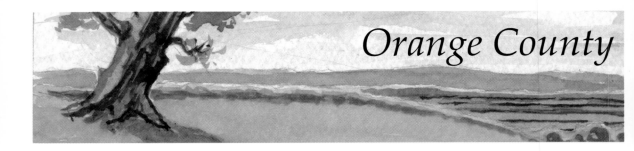
Windfall Farms
Neelytown Road, Montgomery

Pitts's father inherited Windfall Farms, which had been a dairy farm. It lay fallow for years before Pitts finally realized his dream. He started the venture with his sister Kathy, who went on, after many years of hard work, to pursue a career in therapeutic massage.

The Montgomery farm was certified "Organic" for many years, but a drop in federal guidelines led Pitts to abandon the certification.

"Windfall Farms" by Jacqueline Schwab.

"We at Windfall are always ready to describe the growing practices and uphold what I would call a 'purist' standards," says Jacque Schwab, an artist who also works at the farm. "The produce is grown with absolutely no pesticides no chemicals, no fungicides no chemical fertilizers. We feed the chickens only organic, local feed. And we even get organic soil mix when we need a special potting soil amendment," she says.

Pitts has sponsered a biodiesel processor that is fully functioning and used to make the biodiesel to power the tractor on the farm and the refurbished bus in which he transports the produce to the city - and brings home the waste oil from the restaurants to make into biodiesel. That waste oil, Schwab adds, is delivered to the market in a rickshaw!

Morse believes in the idea of eating locally grown food. He's a part of the Pine Bush Farmer's Market this year, and has taken his produce to the Union Square Greenmarket in New York City for 20 years. His produce appears in many upscale restaurants, and he has a loyal client base. This year, he was rated "Excellent" by Zagat.

As people begin to understand the reasons for eating locally, and to respond to them, Pitts applauds. Eating food grown close to home is "more ecologically plausible," he says.

But it's not enough. The open spaces in Orange County are vanishing, gobbled up for development, for industry, for commerce. The long sight of those who love the land, who love the open spaces, who understand what they contribute to the character and economy of the re-

Bounty Cookbook

BBQ SALMON STEAKS WITH HOT MUSTARD
(courtesy of Bob Gaines and Peter Klein on behalf of Windfall Farms)

6 ea. 10 oz   Salmon Steaks, rubbed with olive oil – seasoned with salt and pepper

BBQ Sauce
1/2 c, honey • 2 TB. brown sugar • 1 TB. miso paste • 1 tsp. molasses
2 TB. soy sauce • 1 TB. plum wine • 1 TB. hot mustard
2 each scallion greens • 1 tsp. ginger, minced • 1 TB. cilantro, chopped
2 TB. sesame oil • 1/2 c. peanut oil • 1 TB. rice vinegar

In a bowl whisk together brown sugar, molasses, honey, soy sauce, miso paste, plum wine and mustard, reserve. In a blender, puree scallion, ginger, cilantro, sesame oil, peanut oil and rice vinegar. Whisk blender ingredients into bowl ingredients. Keep at room temperature if using same day or refrigerate–let stand one hour at room temperature before using.

For Hot Mustard Sauce:
2 TB. mustard powder • 2 TB. water • 2 tsp. rice vinegar
2 TB. water • 6 TB. soy bean oil • 1 TB. chopped cilantro

In a bowl, whisk mustard powder and 2 tablespoons water, let stand 15 min. Add rice vinegar and water. Slowly whisk in oil to emulsify. Season with salt and stir in cilantro. Best if used the same day. Keep covered at room temperature.

Heat grill, clean and brush grill with oil. Place salmon steaks on grill and use spatula to flip them. Cook to desired doneness and brush with BBQ sauce before removing from grill. Serve on a bed of Windfall Farms mixed salad greens drizzled with hot mustard sauce. Yield 4 servings

---

gion is overwhelmed by the short sight of profit.

The pressures of encroaching development, pollution and industrial zoning have pushed Pitts to decide to move out of Orange County. He's not sure yet about his destination, but he wants a place that's quieter and with less truck traffic than at his current spot on Neelytown Road. reduced to a UPC code hidden in a warehouse 3,000 miles away."

Jacqueline Schwab is an oil painter living in Pine Bush, New York. She paints with the Wallkill River School. She studied painting at SUNY at New Paltz and the Woodstock School of Art

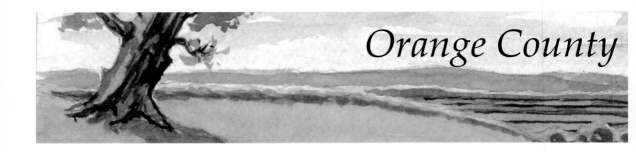

The Blue Parrot
17 Front St.
Port Jervis, NY
(845) 858-1717
www.blueparrotny.com

"Blue Parrot" by Carrie Jacobson.

Bruce Porter grew up in Orange County. Then life took him away. He was living in San Francisco, where he'd developed a love of Mexican food, when he decided it was time to come home. In the daytimes, he works as a stockbroker. The rest of the time, he owns and operates the Blue Parrot, an elegant Mexican restaurant on Front Street in Port Jervis.

What Porter likes best about his role in the restaurant, he says, is creating the ambiance. "The whole feel of it," he says. "It's been called trendy and cosmopolitan. It looks like something from SoHo." He smiles as he speaks, gesturing at the white tablecloths, dark wood and rich colors inside the restaurant.

He also likes the business of building and maintaining the wine list. "People don't necessarily associate wine with Mexican food," he says. But he lived 15 miles outside Napa Valley for 10 years, and "I got really into the wine."

The concept of local foods has taken hold in California, Porter says. It's more than a trend; it's an established fact in many restaurants. The freshness and the quality of the local food just can't be overstated.

Here, he was offered 20 acres on the Neversink in Huguenot. He plans to use it to grow vegetables for the restaurant. Until that project takes hold, he's buying vegetables at the local farmer's market, and using produce grown in his own garden. He also plans to grow mint, cilantro and basil at the restaurant.

The restaurants clustered on the corner of Front and Sussex streets – the Blue Parrot, 20 Front and Port Java – all have taken to the idea of using local foods. This pleases Porter. They're "down with it," he says. "We are, too."

Bounty Cookbook

BLUE PARROT PARTY SALSA for 10
(courtesy of Chef James Devaney)

Dice:
2 big onions • 5 tomatoes • 1 bunch fresh cilantro • 5 fresh jalapenos

Add 8 cups tomato juice • 1 cup ketchup • ½ (half cup) cup sugar
2TB fresh oregano • 3TB salt

Mix together and chill. Serve with chips (try buying tortillas, cutting them into chip shapes and frying instead of using packaged chips) – or use as garnish.

MEXICAN CHILI for 10

5 cups chopped meat (top round is a good choice)
3 TB fresh garlic, chopped • ½ (half-cup) cup chopped onions

Saute with ¼ (quarter-cup) cup oil until meat is browned. Add 1 1/2 (one and a half cups) cups diced tomatoes, simmer for 5 minutes.

In blender, blend
3 cloves • 4 fresh garlic cloves • ½ (one-half) TB cumin
5 chilis de arbol (you can find these in Mexican grocery stores)

Blend, add to meat, simmer 5 more minutes. Add ¼ cup (a quarter-cup) tequila
1 cup orange juice and ½ (one-half cup) cup tomato paste. Simmer 10 more minutes.

Along with its elegance, the restaurant has an edge of easy charm. The blue parrot itself, displayed on the turquoise and white flags that hang above the restaurant's entryway, was designed by Porter's 7-year-old daughter, Lily. The cook, Hugo Mendez, makes everything from scratch, with the exception of the chilis relenos.   His mother, Sara Martinez, comes in regularly to make these.

Carrie Jacobson came to painting when she was 50; she felt it was her soul singing out. People enjoy her landscapes and her paintings of dogs and cats, her favorite subjects.

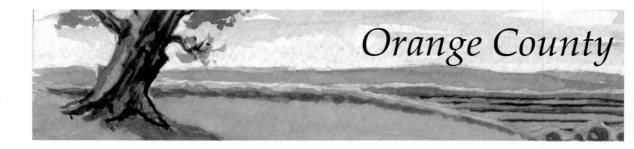

Mead-Tooker House B&B
136 Clinton St.
Montgomery, NY 12549
(845) 457-5770
www.meadtooker.com

"Mead-Tooker House" Pastel
by Shawn Dell Joyce.

Edward Devitt II has heard his soul sing, and joined in the chorus.

Two and a half years ago, he opened Mead-Tooker House, a bed and breakfast in Montgomery. "Hospitality management runs deep in my bones and I truly love it!" he says, exclamation mark and all.

The Mead-Tooker House, listed on the National Register of Historic Houses, began as three separate houses, which were eventually attached. The structure went up, of course, in stages, starting in the late 1700s. The B&B has eight guest rooms, most of which have working fireplaces.

The B&B offers breakfast, snacks and tea. Innkeeper Devitt says the best part of being the chef is that he gets to hear the wonderful things people say about what he prepares for them.

Eating locally is important, Devitt believes. It supports the local farms, and this "has to be one of the best ways we can all contribute to the wealth of our community."

Whenever possible, Devitt says, the Mead-Tooker B&B supports and buys from local farms.

"In 1801, the world's first discovery of an extinct creature happened in Montgomery by artist/scientist Charles Willson Peale. The Montgomery Mastodon is commemorated in a mural by artist Shawn Dell Joyce hanging in Montgomery Town Hall on Bracken Road."

Bounty Cookbook

EASY HONEY BARBEQUE CHICKEN DRUMSTICKS
(courtesy of Mead-Tooker House B&B)

4-5 lbs. chicken legs (skin on or off)
Seasoning salt
Pepper
Oil (for frying)
2 lg onions (chopped)
1-2 tbls fresh minced garlic
2 medium green bell peppers, seeded and sliced (optional)
2 8 ounce cans tomato sauce
1/2 cup cider vinegar
1/2 cup honey
1/4 cup brown sugar (optional)
1-2 tablespoons prepared yellow mustard (optional)
1/4 cup Worcestershire sauce
2-4 teaspoons paprika
Hot pepper sauce

Season chicken legs with seasoning salt and pepper. In a frying pan with oil, brown the chicken legs on all sides.

Place the chicken legs in a greased casserole dish. Sprinkle with chopped onions and garlic.

In a bowl, combine all remaining ingredients, mix well, and pour over the chicken. Bake at 350 degrees for about 40-45 minutes. Yield 3-5 servings

"Artifacts dating before the Ice Age (12,000 years ago) were found at the Town Park at Benedict Farm in Montgomery along the Wallkill River, making it one of the longest populated areas in Orange County."

Shawn Dell Joyce is a sustainable artist and activist, founder of the Wallkill River School, and writes a syndicated weekly column called "Sustainable Living" in the Sunday Times Herald Record. She has works in major museum collections, and private collections around the world. www.WallkillRiverSchool.com

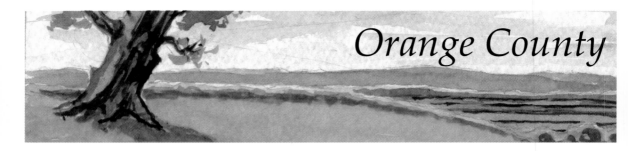
Phillies Bridge Farm Project
Gardiner NY

Located on a beautiful and historic 65 acre farm 5 miles south of New Paltz, in Gardiner, NY, Phillies Bridge Farm Project (PBFP) is a not-for-profit corporation with the primary purpose of education on multiple issues surrounding healthy food production. PBFP provides direct experiences of food, farming, and the cycles of nature. Since 1995 we have worked to promote Hudson Valley agriculture that is ecologically sound, community oriented, and economically viable.

Community Supported Agriculture is a direct relationship between farmer and eater. You join a CSA by purchasing a "share" at a fixed cost at the beginning of the season. As a shareholder, you then receive an assortment of produce grown and freshly harvested by your friendly local farmer. By paying up front at the start of the season, you are supporting a local farm by guaranteeing a market for the produce, and by providing income to purchase seeds, tools, and equipment for that season.

In exchange, you receive a seasonal variety of beautiful, delicious, lovingly grown vegetables. You reap the rewards of a bountiful harvest, but you also assume the risks of possible crop damage caused by good old Nature. The CSA relationship is a friendly and personally gratifying way to buy vegetables, and one that connects you with the people and the land that grow your food.

"Skytop from Phillies Bridge Farm" by Shawn Dell Joyce.

CSA shareholders at Phillies Bridge Farm Project subscribe in the spring and receive fresh, locally-grown produce once a week from early June to mid-November. Pick-up is at the farm (located just south of New Paltz of off Hwy 208) on Tuesdays from 4 to 7 PM or Saturdays from 9 AM to 12 PM. Provided enrollment is high enough, we also drop-off on Saturdays from 11 AM to 1 PM in Rosendale and Kingston. Phillies Bridge Farm Project CSA uses organic farming practices, and does not support the use of chemical fertilizers, pesticides, or herbicides. We strive for agricultural practices which are environmentally low-impact and foster diverse ecosystems on our land.

Bounty Cookbook

LINGUINI GREMOLATA
(courtesy of Phillies Bridge Farm)

1/2 lb. zucchini (one large or two small; other squash can be substituted
1-1/2 c. cherry tomatoes
3 cloves of garlic, pressed
2 tsp. lemon zest
2 TB. parsley
3 TB. olive oil
1-1/2 tsp. salt
1/8 tsp. pepper
1/2 lb. linguine
2 TB. pine nuts
fresh basil leaves
grated parmesan

"View from Phillies Bridge" by Mary Sealfon.

To make the gremolata; combine the garlic, lemon zest and parsley; set aside. Cook pasta per directions. In a sauté pan, heat olive oil and sauté squash with garlic, salt and pepper. Add 1/2 cup boiling pasta water to the squash with cherry tomatoes. Cook for a few minutes, then toss with gremolata. Spoon onto plates and grate a bit of parmesan and a few sliced basil leaves and pine nuts.

We encourage shareholders to visit the farm to experience the changing of the seasons and enjoy the open space and stunning views. We welcome volunteer participation as well; working alongside the farmers and interns builds connections between your family and our farm and allows you to have a hand in growing your own food!

Shawn Dell Joyce is a sustainable artist and activist, founder of the Wallkill River School, and writes a syndicated weekly column called "Sustainable Living" in the Sunday Times Herald Record. She has works in major museum collections, and private collections around the world. www.WallkillRiverSchool.com

Mary Mugele Sealfon received a BA in painting at the U of California at Santa Barbara and a MA from NYU. In New York City she pursued a career as an Art Director and designer. She has won numerous awards and her paintings and prints have been exhibited nationally and internationally. She also teaches art locally, including SUNY Orange.

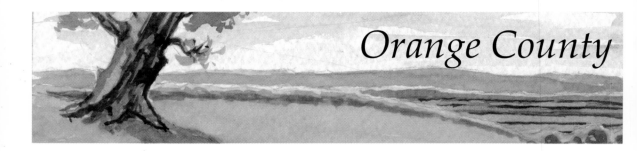

D'Attolico Organic Farm
Warwick Farmers' Market

Vincent D'Attolico's father emigrated from Italy as one of nine children searching for a better life. Vincent credits his grandmother with instilling traditional farming techniques (no chemicals) into his dad who began farming at age 9. Vincent and his parents moved to their Black Dirt region farm when he was just 13. Young Vincent was not too eager to give up the fun of being a teen for the rigors of farming.

"The Farmers' Life" by John Creagh

"While working one day I realized that I could eat anything on the farm because it wasn't sprayed with chemicals," says Vincent. He was dismayed that farm workers had to wear special suits and masks to spray the fields of other farms.

Vincent and his wife Denise began farming the same land in 1976. Determined to keep his grandmother's teachings alive and farm the "way it was intended." The D'Attolicos have a two year old daughter Clairice who eats vegetables and raspberries right out of the fields. Her parents know that she "is eating the best and safest food anywhere." As do the D'Atolicos loyal customers.

"Our customers prefer super fresh food, and want to know where it came from," notes Vincent. He helped to found the Warwick Farmers Market where you can find his booth every Sunday during the growing season. "People who buy from local farms are ensuring that our country has food security," noted Vincent. "Some foreign food exporters grow food in harmful chemicals and unsanitary conditions. Without local farms, there would be no choice."

Bounty Cookbook

VEGGIE STIR FRY
(courtesy of Vincent and Denise D'Attolico)

1 small onion chopped
1 leek sliced
3 cloves garlic, pressed
1 stalk celery, chopped
1 medium zucchini, chopped
1 medium carrot, chopped
1 container sprouted lentils, mung beans or sunflower sprouts from local farm
2 TB. olive oil
1 TB. butter
1/2 c. chicken broth

Heat olive oil and butter in a wok or fry pan. Add onion, leek and garlic; sauté for 2-3 minutes. Add carrots, celery, zucchini and chicken broth. Cook on medium heat for 8 minutes, stirring occasionally. Add sprouts and toss. Serve immediately.
 Yield 6 servings

ROASTED PLUM TOMATOES AND PASTA

2 lbs. mini plum tomatoes from local farms cut in half lengthwise
5 cloves garlic, pressed
olive oil
salt
package of cooked pasta

Lay cut tomatoes in a roasting pan, drizzle with olive oil, pressed garlic and salt. Mix together with your hands, then spread tomatoes into a single layer. Roast in 200 degree oven for 45 minutes and serve over pasta.

John Creagh has been a painter and an instructor for over 25 years, as well as a member and instructor for the Wallkill River School. His artwork is featured in many private collections around the world, you can visit him at www.jcreagh.com

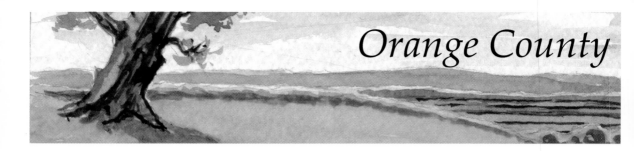

Winding Hills Golf Club & Restaurant
1847 State Route 17K
Montgomery
845-457-3187
www.WindingHillsGolfCourse.com

2007 marks the ten year anniversary of this family-owned golf course and restaurant. Founded by Edward and Marc Devitt, the golf course is the culmination of many Devitt family passions; it sits on an historic home-stead site, has a picturesque view of a tree-lined 18 hole fairway, and offers four-star fare in the restaurant and dining patio.

"Afternoon Tea Time" by Linda Richichi.

The Restaurant at Winding Hills Golf Course is rated as "One of the Hudson Valley's Top Ten Restaurants." The menu features contemporary American favorites like crab cakes, wraps and salads to more elegant Poached Salmon , and Chicken Marsala for catered events and weddings. Fresh herbs are grown on the golf course in one of the many seasonal gardens. These herbs are used to flavor most dishes.

The golf course is an 18 hole executive course that is open to the public from April through November everyday from 7am to dusk. Many of the stone wall fences are original to the historic property which encompasses the ruins of a colonial home, a hand-dug well capped with a Walt Whitman poem, and a pond with a spectacular waterfall.

"As a family-owned and operated business, we take great pride in our golf course and restaurant, in the quality of our service and in insuring our guests enjoy their experience with us." Notes Ed Devitt.

Bounty Cookbook

GRILLED GARDEN VEGETABLES WITH PENNE PASTA
(courtesy of Winding Hills Golf Club & Restaurant)

1 zucchini
1/2 red onion
1 green pepper
2 cloves garlic
1/2 cherry tomatoes, halved
1 c. fresh mozzarella
1 lb. sweet Italian sausage
1/4 c. parmesan cheese
1/4 c. fresh basil
1/4 c. fresh parsley
salt and pepper
olive oil
1 lb. penne pasta

"Garlic & Tomatoes " by William Noonan.

Begin by slicing red onion into 1/2 inch slices. Slice zucchini in half lengthwise. Cut the pepper into quarters and remove seeds and membranes. Brush vegetables with olive oil and season with salt and pepper. Grill vegetables to your liking and cut into bite size pieces. Set vegetables aside. In a large skillet or grill, cook sausage until brown. Cut cooked sausage into bit size pieces. In large pot, bring water to a rolling boil, add salt and pasta and cook for 8-10 minutes. Drain. Dice fresh mozzarella into 1/2 inch cubes and chop the basil and parsley. Toss all and serve. Yield 4 servings

Locally born international artist Linda Richichi creates plein air paintings of the spiritual energy of nature. Awards include the "Best In Show" at the fourth annual IPAP Worldwide Paint Out in Niagara Falls, Ontario. Her work is included in private, corporate and museum collections internationally. Her studio is in Newburgh, NY and is open by appointment. www.LindaRichichi.com.

William Noonan is a artist who resides and works in Orange County. He is known for his loose brushwork and sophisticated use of color. You can see examples of his work on his website at www.williamnoonan.com.

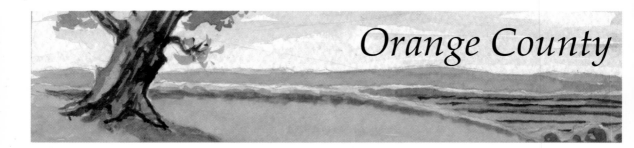

Harmony Farm
144 Broadlea Road
Goshen NY
(845) 294-3181
www.harmony-farm.org

Even while Hubert McCabe was growing up in Norwalk, Conn., he wanted to be a farmer. He planted things, tended them, watched them grow. Every year, he would visit his father's family in Ireland, and work on the family dairy farm.

"Harmony Farm" by Carrie Jacobson.

For a time, life got in the way of wishes, though. McCabe, city boy, son of an Irish immigrant, went to college. He went on to earn a master's degree in social work. He started to work with kids in the Bronx, kids who needed him. The job burned him out.

He was about to take a year off when he heard about Harmony Farm. The farm, a couple acres, is part of about 150 acres in Goshen, owned by the Dominican Sisters of Blauvelt, NY, and leased to, among others, the Highbridge Community Life Center. Highbridge runs social programs in the city, and uses the Empowerment Center, a lovely stone building on the Goshen acreage, as a retreat center. Kids come up from the city, get involved, maybe see a different horizon, a different future.

McCabe cut the social work back to three days a week, and set out to be a part-time farmer in Goshen three days a week. Two and a half years later, he dropped the social work.

"This," he says, looking around, " is all about potential. And then we get to eat the solution."

Surrounded by a high deer fence, Harmony Farm sits on a sunny hillside that looks out over hills and mountains and more farms. It's a CSA, with working memberships as an option. The membership has grown dramatically, say McCabe and Greg Henderson, who also works there.

Harmony has 69 members now, nearly no turnover, and a long waiting list. McCabe is petitioning to expand.

Bounty Cookbook

CURRIED RICE MOLD
(courtesy of Orange County Tourism)

2 cup rice
4 cup water
2 bullion cubes (any flavor preference)
1 cup broken raw linguini
1 teaspoon minced garlic
1 tablespoon olive oil
1 medium green pepper diced
1 medium red pepper diced
4 diced scallions (including greens)
2 cans artichoke cut into small pieces
1-1/4 teaspoon curry
1/2 cup diced zucchini, unpeeled

"Along the Indian Road" by Laura Martinez-Bianco

Cook rice in water flavored with bullion. Set aside to cool. Heat olive oil with garlic; add linguini broken into 1-1/2" pieces – brown until linguini is darkened. Set aside. Combine all remaining ingredients in large bowl. Toss in rice and linguini. Mix thoroughly and pack into deep mixing bowl that is lightly sprayed with cooking spray. Chill 3-4 hours. Unmold onto bed of lettuce garnished with cherry tomatoes or other fresh raw vegetables. Yields 6-8 servings

"We can't grow fast enough," he says. "There's so much more demand than supply."

According to the website, the farm uses use biodynamic practices based on the spiritual insights of the Austrian scientist-philosopher, Rudolf Steiner. This recognizes the soil as a living organism, and works to strengthen it and correct imbalances. Harmony Farm also uses sound organic practices, crop rotations and careful tillage. Chemical pesticides, fungicides, fertilizers and herbicides are not used.

Eating local is at the heart of Harmony Farm. "It's always better to buy it from your neighbor."

Carrie Jacobson came to painting when she was 50; she felt it was her soul singing out. People enjoy her landscapes and her paintings of dogs and cats, her favorite subjects.

Laura Martinez-Bianco is a plein air painter who works throughout the Hudson Valley capturing the light and color of a specific moment. As well as working in the Hudson Valley, Laura has traveled to Europe and Canada to paint. Laura's studio and gallery space, is located at 384 Bingham Road, Marlboro, NY and is open by appointment. www.laurabianco.com <http://www.laurabianco.com>

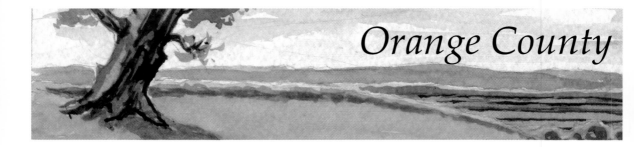

Pacific Restaurant
North Main Street
Harriman, NY

Darrel Lexandra lives in Harriman, and he
loves the town. After September 11, he opened
Angelo's, a small, family-run Italian restaurant,
in Harriman. He's had time to think. And when
he looked around recently, looked around at
the town that is the focus of his life, he saw it
was lacking something - a seafood restaurant
and sushi bar.

So, he set about to fill the need, and on Sept.
12, 2007, he opened Pacific Restaurant.

The best part about it, he says, is "using the
best ingredients available and watching our
guests enjoying what we created."

"Pacific", by Bruce Thorne

Eating locally means freshness and tastiness, for sure.
But for Lexandra, it also means keeping the revenue in the community, so it can be recycled
back into the community again and again. "Helping everyone!" he says.

And, asked what he'd like his Orange County neighbors to know about him, he says,
"Although our resturants (Angelo's and Pacific) are located in the wonderful Hamlet of
Harriman, we are as good as, and in most cases better than, anything in NYC."

"Harriman State Park has over 32 lakes,
and 40 marked trails making it
one of the largest in NY State.."

SPICY FRIED CALAMARI SALAD
(courtesy of Pacific Restaurant)

1/4 cup flour
5 oz calamari, cut
1 oz mustard greens
1/4 head red leaf
1/4 green leaf
1/3 head romaine
1 tomato
1/4 Red onion
1 lemon
2oz Extra Virgin Olive Oil
Pinch of Salt
Pinch of Pepper
Red Crushed Pepper, to taste
6-7 Sicilian Green Olives, pitted

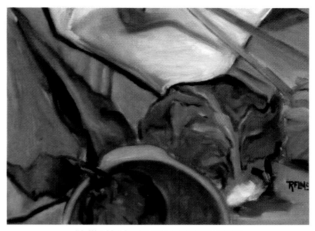
"Still Life" by Ronnie Mehrberg-Lipitz

Dredge cut Calamri rings in flour. Fry until golden brown. Toss all greens in large bowl, add slices of lemon (circles), olives and onions, salt, pepper and red crusted pepper (to taste). Add 1/4 cup extra virgin olive oil and juice of 1/2 lemon and warm Calamari and serve. Yield 1 serving

"Brotherhood Winery in Washingtonville was built in 1839, and is the oldest continuously operating winery in the nation."

Bruce Thorne-His style has been compared to Van Gogh for his rich color, thick impasto paint technique and his passion for painting.

Ronnie Mehrberg Lipitz-A Former High School art teacher. Studied art at Adelphi University, Pratt, Parsons, FIT, and SVA. She is currently painting at the Art Students' League and with The Wallkill River School of Painting. She resides in New York City and In Sugarloaf, N.Y.

FRESH BLUEBERRY PIE
(courtesy of Penny Thelman)

9 inch pie pan
1 pie crust (see recipe below)
4 c. blueberries (mix of wild and
    cultivated berries is great)
1 c. sugar (if using wild blueberries
use 1-1/2 cups sugar)
3 TB. cornstarch
1/3 c. cold water
1/4 tsp. cinnamon (may add more
    if preferred)
1/2 tsp. lemon or orange juice

"Blueberry Pie" by Penny Thelman who is a watercolorist from Wolf Lake. She is very active in the lake community as well as the Wurtsboro arts community. She has been a member of the Wallkill River School.

In saucepan place 3 cups of berries, sugar, cinnamon and juice. Heat this mixture on the stove top over medium heat, stirring gently until mixture starts to simmer. In a separate bowl or cup mix the cornstarch and water together and stir until dissolved. Add the mixture to the saucepan. Bring the mixture back up to a simmer and stir continuously for 3 to 5 minute or until the blueberry mixture thickens and becomes clear. Remove from heat and let cool at room temperature for 5 minutes. Add the remaining cup of blueberries to the saucepan and gently mix. Pour into pie crust. Let the pie sit and cool to room temperature before serving.

<u>Pie Crust</u>
1 c. flour • 1/3 c. shortening • 1/4 tsp. salt • 4 to 5 TB. cold water

Heat oven to 375 degrees. Place flour and salt in a bowl and gently stir. Cut in part of the shortening with a fork or pastry knife. After the mixture resembles breadcrumbs cut in the remaining shortening. Add the cold water 1 tablespoon at a time while mixing it into the flour. Only moisten and work a portion of the dough at a time until the dough sticks together. Try to work the dough as little as possible. Form the dough into a ball and place it on a floured surface; roll it out to fit the pan. Place the crust into the pie pan and flute the top so that the crust extends over the top of the pan. Take a fork and gently prick the bottom and sides of the crust several times. (This allows the steam to vent while the crust is baking.) Bake at 375 for 15 to 20 minutes or until the crust is golden. Remove from the oven and let the crust cool before adding in the filing.

Bounty Cookbook

SOUTHWESTERN ALFREDO WITH PENNE
(courtesy of Pat Morgan)

6-8 oz. boneless chicken breasts cut into bite size pieces or strips
1 TB. butter plus 1 tbs olive oil
2 cloves garlic
1 tsp. crushed red pepper (optional)
1/4 c. sun dried tomatoes (cut in slivers)
1/2 chopped onion
1/2 chopped green pepper
1 TB. Bacos or cooked crumbled bacon
1 TB. basil
1 c. sliced mushrooms
1 c. tomato sauce (your own or prepared)
1/2 c. half and half
2-3 TB. parmesan cheese
16oz. penne pasta

In large skillet, sauté chicken in butter and oil. (Do not overcook) Remove to separate bowl. In same pan, sauté garlic, tomatoes, onion, peppers and mushrooms. Add chicken and remaining ingredients and simmer on low heat until pasta is cooked. Drain pasta; pour into large bowl and pour sauce on top. Sprinkle with parmesan cheese. Yield 4 servings

Notes: You can vary ingredients such as onions, zucchini, broccoli, fresh tomatoes. Try Fat Free Half & Half as a healthy version of Alfredo. Recipe doubles well.

*"West Point boasts notable graduates
like Civil War General Robert E. Lee in 1829,
Astronaut Buzz Aldrin in 1951, and former president
Dwight D. Eisenhower in 1915."*

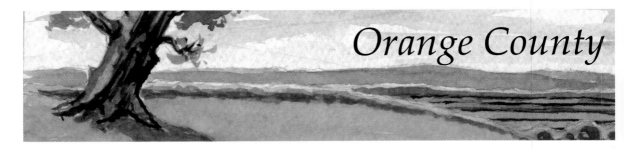

CHICKEN CATALINA
(courtesy of Pat Morgan)

6-8 oz. boneless chicken cut into bite size chunks.
1 small bottle Catalina Fat Free salad dressing
1 envelope Onion Soup mix.
1 large onion chopped
1 green pepper chopped in large chunks
1 clove fresh garlic chopped
1 pkg fresh mushrooms, sliced
1/2 c. walnuts or pecans (large broken pieces)

"Potted Plant" by Pat Morgan.

Place chicken in shallow baking dish. Sprinkle onion, pepper, garlic, mushrooms and nuts over chicken. Combine salad dressing and soup mix and pour over all. Bake covered at 350 about 45-50 minutes. Serve over rice or noodles.

CUCUMBER AND CILANTRO SAUCE
(courtesy of Pat Morgan)

1 cucumber peeled, seeded, chopped finely
1/2 cup chopped cilantro
1 tablespoon Lime juice
salt and pepper to taste
1 cup fat free plain yogurt

Combine first 4 ingredients. Add the yogurt slowly to make a thick chunky sauce. Chill. Serve over salmon or chicken. Lasts for several days in air tight container.

Pat Morgan, a watercolor painter, has studied with artists including Richard Ochs, Eli Rosenthal and Mel Stabin. Currently, she is represented by the Wallkill River Gallery. She has received local and regional awards for her work, and enjoys teaching other painters her love of watercolor.

PASTA A LA CAPRESE WITH MOZZARELLA
Marge Corriere, Blooming Hill Farm, Blooming Grove NY

1 lb ziti or rigatoni (preferably whole wheat pasta for the flavor and health benefits)
4-5 large fresh heirloom tomatoes, sliced
5 smashed cloves garlic
20 leaves fresh basil – sliced thinly
1/2 c. extra virgin olive oil
1 tsp. salt
 freshly ground pepper
8 oz. mozzarella cubed
grated Parmigianna-romano

Mix together all ingredients except pasta and grated cheese. Let sit for a few hours on the kitchen counter. The cheese will start to get soft and almost melted looking, and the other ingredients will become fragrant and juicy. Cook the pasta according to package directions, drain and return to hot pot. Toss the pasta and the sauce over low heat for about three minutes, just until the cheese starts to melt and spread. Put in a serving bowl and add grated cheese. Serve with a fresh green salad and you have a summer feast to remember. Yields 4-6 servings.

"Brotherhood Winery in Washingtonville
was built in 1839, and is the
oldest continuously operating winery
in the nation."

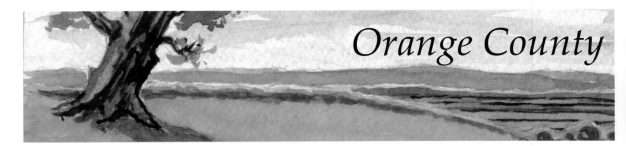

BEEF STEW
(courtesy Pablo Rosado, Chef, Flik Independence Schools)

4 lbs. beef shank or chuck, cut into cubes
1/2 tsp. salt
1/2 tsp. pepper   1 oz. vegetable oil
3 of each, carrots, celery, onions; chopped
2 oz. tomato paste
2-1/2 oz. flour
1 qt. beef broth
1 bunch fresh parsley stems

Garnish:
4 oz. peas
20 each carrots, celery, turnips,
        pearl onions, cubed

"Phillies Bridge Goat" by Lisa O'Gorman Hoffsomer.

Season the beef with salt and pepper and sear in hot oil. Remove and reserve. Add carrots, celery and onions; let the onions brown. Add tomato paste and cook out for several seconds. Add flour to carrots, celery and onions. Cook out the roux. Add one-third of stock; whip out the lumps and bring to a simmer. Add remaining stock and return to simmer; add parsley. Cover beef and braise in oven until very tender. Cook vegetables for garnish separately until very tender; reserve. Degrease the stew; discard stems. Adjust seasoning with salt and pepper to taste; reheat the garnish. Serve stew garnished with vegetables. Yield 10 servings.

"Tuxedo Park is the namesake of the Tuxedo dinner jacket designed by tobacco magnate Pierre Lorillard."

Lisa O'Gorman-Hofsommer was born & raised in Yonkers, N.Y. She moved to the Hudson Valley in 1990. She has been painting in pastels since then, and has strong desire to paint wildlife & landscapes. She has a Pet Portraits business. <Petportraitsnmore.com>

Bounty Cookbook

BOUNTY MEAT BALLS
(courtesy of Ellen Trayer)

2 lb. Hudson Valley ground beef
1 McCoun apple -- grated
1/2 c. breadcrumbs
1 onion -- chopped
1 egg -- lightly beaten
1 clove garlic -- crushed
2 tsp. caraway
2 tsp. Worcestershire sauce
2 cans beef broth
salt and pepper to taste

Combine meat, apple, breadcrumbs, onion, egg, garlic, salt and pepper and form meatballs. Brown and pour off all but 2 tablespoons of fat. Blend 2 tablespoons of flour into fat and brown lightly. Add 2 cans beef broth and stir until smooth and thick. Add caraway, Worcestershire, salt and pepper. Return meatballs and simmer for 10 minutes. Serve with mashed potatoes or over rice.

"Orange County Farm" by Bruce Thorne

Bruce Thorne-His style has been compared to Van Gogh for his rich color, thick impasto paint technique and his passion for painting.

SPICED PEACH SHORTCAKE
(courtesy of Lee Ann Schwope, The former Dairy Pricess)

2 c. all purpose flour
1/2 c. packed brown sugar
1 TB. Baking powder
2 tsp. pumpkin pie spice
1/2 tsp. salt
1/2 c. butter
3/4 c. buttermilk (or put 1 tsp. lemon juice or vinegar in regular milk and
      let it sit 5 mins.)
2 eggs
4 c. sliced peaches
1/4 c. plus 2 TBS. sugar divided
1 c. whipping cream
1 tsp vanilla

"Peaches" by Neil Granholm

Preheat oven to 375 degrees. Butter a 9" round pan.
In a medium bowl, combine flour, brown sugar, baking powder, pumpkin pie spice, and salt. Cut in butter until mixture resembles coarse crumbles. Add buttermilk and eggs, stirring until ingredients are moistened. Spread batter in pan. Bake 25-30 mins. Cool on a wire rack. In a large bowl, combine peaches with sugar, cover and refrigerate 30 mins. Whip cream with remaining 2 TBS of sugar and vanilla until stiff peaks form. Split cooled shortcake in half horizontally, top with 1/2 the whipped cream and 1/2 the peaches, and repeat. Serve immediately.

"Horace Pippin, one of the best known primitive artists in America lived and worked in Goshen."

Neil Granholm was well known for his colorful abstract compositions before joining the Wallkill River School. He is now an accomplished oil painter, a fine woodworker, and a member of many regional arts organizations.

Bounty Cookbook

ROASTED VEGETABLE MEDLEY
(courtesy of Virginia Redman)

2 large peeled potatoes cut into wedges
1 yam or sweet potato peeled and cut into wedges
3 carrots cut into 1/2 in. pieces
3 parsnips peeled and cut into 1/2 in. pieces
1 green squash sliced into 1/2 in. rings
1 yellow squash sliced into 1/2 in. rings
1 red onion peeled but into 8 wedges
1 cup green beans broken in half

"Weeds Barn" by Laura Martinez-Bianco

Mix all ingredients. Bake in 9 x 13 greased dish. Drizzle all over with olive oil. Add 3 sprigs of rosemary, salt and pepper to taste. Bake one hour at 400 degrees until browned and tender. Yield 6 servings

"Orange County's greatest land speculator, William Henry Seward was born in the village of Florida in 1801. Seward was wounded by a would-be assassin on the same night that Lincoln was murdered. After his recovery, Seward remained in the administration of Andrew Johnson and at that time negotiated with Russia for the purchase of the vast frozen wilderness known as Alaska in 1867. At that time, the soon-to-be-state was known as "Seward's Folly" for the seemingly bad deal that Seward made."

Laura Martinez-Bianco is a plein air painter who works throughout the Hudson Valley capturing the light and color of a specific moment. As well as working in the Hudson Valley, Laura has traveled to Europe and Canada to paint. Laura's studio and gallery space, is located at 384 Bingham Road, Marlboro, NY and is open by appointment. www.laurabianco.com <http://www.laurabianco.com>

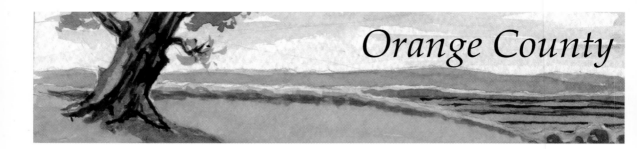

STUFFED ZUCCHINI
(courtesy of Sharon Tompkins)

zucchini
onion
tomato
egg
breadcrumbs
parmesan cheese
oregano, salt, pepper
butter

"Heirloom Squash" by Shawn Dell Joyce

Halve a small zucchini, scrape out, leaving rim.

Saute small onion in butter. Add the pulp chopped. Quarter a tomato (with skin removed) add to pan. Separately beat 1 egg, 1/2 cup breadcrumbs, 1/2 cup parmesan cheese. Mix and add to pan mixture. Add oregano, salt and pepper to taste. Spread zucchini rims with butter. Pour in stuffing. Place zucchini rims in baking dish and add a little water to pan.

Bake 30 minutes in 350 oven, uncovered. Brown tops in broiler. Yield 2-4 servings

"Downing Park features a commanding view of the Hudson River from its central hilltop. It was designed in 1887 by Frederick Law Olmstead and Calvert Vaux at no charge. The legendary landscape architects also designed Central Park in Manhattan."

Shawn Dell Joyce is a sustainable artist and activist, founder of the Wallkill River School, and writes a syndicated weekly column called "Sustainable Living" in the Sunday Times Herald Record. She has works in major museum collections, and private collections around the world. www.WallkillRiverSchool.com

Bounty Cookbook

PARSLEY SOUP
(courtesy of Ruth A. Kahn)

4 oz. bunch parsley, washed
2 onions chopped
2 potatoes, cubed
2 oz. butter
1 quart (4 cups) chicken stock or soup
salt and pepper to taste

Cut parsley stalks off and set aside. Sweat the chopped onions and potatoes in the butter for 6 min. till soft. Tie the stalks into bundle and add to stock with onions and potatoes. Cook for 10-15 minutes – remove stalks and toss away. Pour into a blender together with parsley tops until parsley is quite fine. Season. Serve hot or cold.
Yield 2-4servings

"Pine Hill Road Sign" by Marge Morales

"Greenwood Lake was once described in travel brochures as the "Switzerland of New York." In the late 1800's and for years to come, it became a popular destination with many fine resorts located along its shores."

Marge Morales of Rock Tavern sees herself as a modern-day storyteller, using paint as her medium. In oils and watercolors, Marge offers more than images; her art tells stories that touch the heart and the soul.

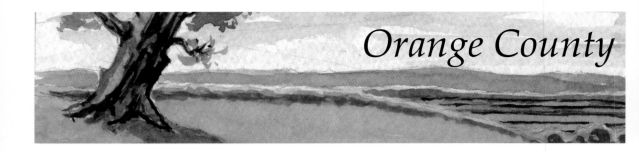

BARLEY SALAD
(courtesy of Orange County Tourism)

The great thing about this recipe is that it is very versatile and can accept lots of different substitutions. I originally got the recipe from Food Network but have been reworking it for the past few years. Great substitute for rice or potatoes.

3-4 tablespoons orange juice of pineapple juice
2 tablespoons extra virgin olive oil
3-1/2-4 cup cooked and cooled barley
1 small head fennel, julienned (use just the stalks)
1/2 red pepper –optional
1/2 diced onion – optional
1/4 cup pine nuts toasted or hazelnuts or plain almonds
1/2 cup parmesan or Romano cheese, grated
1/2 cup cooked and crumbled bacon or pancetta
2 tablespoons chopped fresh parley or mint leaves
freshly ground black pepper and kosher salt

In a small bowl, whisk together the juice and a pinch of kosher salt. Add the olive oil and whisk to combine. Set aside. Combine the remaining ingredients in a large mixing bowl. Add the dressing and stir to combine. Season, to taste, with salt and pepper. Serve immediately or allow to sit in the refrigerator for up to 1 hour.

"Bear Mountain State Park was named because
the profile of the mountain resembles a bear lying down.
It welcomes more visitors every year than
Yellowstone National Park."

Bounty Cookbook

WHITE BEAN SPREAD WITH SPINACH & RED PEPPERS
(courtesy of Barbara Wyman)

4 c. baby spinach
1 can (15 oz) white beans, rinsed and drained
1-2 TB. fat-free, reduced sodium chicken or vegetable broth
1 TB. extra virgin olive oil
1 TB. freshly squeezed lemon juice
1-2 cloves garlic, peeled and crushed
salt and pepper to taste
1/4 c. fresh parsley, chopped
1/2 c. red onion, minced (optional)
1/2 c. grated carrots
1 jar (7 oz) roasted red peppers packed in water, drained and chopped
paprika for garnish (optional)

In a nonstick skillet over medium-high heat, sauté the spinach with a pinch of salt, stirring constantly until wilted 3 to 4 minutes. Set aside to cool. In a food processor, puree beans with broth, olive oil, lemon juice, garlic, salt and pepper. Add parsley and pulse until combined. Spread half of the bean mixture onto a serving plate, smoothing the top flat. Layer the spinach evenly on top of the beans and sprinkle on the onion and carrots. Top with a layer of roasted red peppers. Spread remaining bean puree over red peppers. Sprinkle with paprika if desired and serve with whole wheat pita wedges.

"One of Orange County's most successful artist families is the Goulds. John F. Gould established the Bethlehem Art Gallery and Art School in 1957 located near Newburgh, NY. He was a prominent illustrator for the Saturday Evening Post for more than eight years and an illustrator for many national corporations, two of his sons; Paul (artist) and William (photographer) are still working artists in Orange County."

CURRIED FRUITED CHICKEN SALAD
(courtesy of Michelle Filer)

2 chicken breasts, cooked and diced
1/4 c. chopped onion
1 small apple or pear, chopped
1/3 c. raisins
1/3 c. chopped nuts, pecan or walnut
1/2 c. light mayo
1/4-1/2 tsp. curry powder
salt and pepper to taste

Mix all ingredients to coat.

"Pears" by Mary Evelyn Whitehill

TOMATO BASIL SALAD
(courtesy of Pat Morgan)

3 large tomatoes, chopped in medium chunks
4-5 fresh basil leaves (chiffonade - stack on top of each other, roll up and slice thinly)
1/4 c. low fat raspberry salad dressing
salt and pepper to taste

Combine all ingredients and stir. The following can be added for variety; walnuts, pecans, dried cranberries, chickpeas.

Mary Evelyn Whitehill has over 27 years of watercolor experience and is a demonstrating artist for the Wallkill River School. She is also the great-granddaughter of Hudson River School artist Thomas Pope. www.mewhitehill.com

Bounty Cookbook

JILL'S SUPPER SQUASH ERADICATION RECIPE
(courtesy of Jill MacElhiney, Huguenot Farm CSA)

1/3 c. plus 1/4 c. extra-virgin olive oil
5 large zucchini (about 2 pounds), cut into 1/4-inch rounds
Salt and freshly ground black pepper
3 garlic cloves, thinly sliced
1/4 c. chopped fresh basil leaves
1/4 c. chopped fresh mint leaves
10 medium carrots (about 1 pound), peeled and cut into 1/4-inch rounds
1/4 c. red wine vinegar

Heat 1/3 cup oil in a heavy large frying pan over medium-high heat. Working in batches, add the zucchini and fry until golden, about 2 minutes per side. Using a slotted spoon, transfer the fried zucchini to a baking dish. Sprinkle generously with salt and pepper. Sprinkle half of the garlic, basil, and mint leaves over the zucchini. Add the remaining oil to the frying pan. Add the carrots to the hot oil and sauté until golden, about 5 minutes. Using a slotted spoon, transfer the fried carrots to the dish of zucchini. Sprinkle generously with salt and pepper. Sprinkle the remaining garlic, basil, and mint leaves over. Drizzle the vinegar over the vegetable mixture and toss gently to coat. Cool to room temperature. Cover and marinate in the refrigerator overnight. Allow the vegetables to come to room temperature before serving.

Lee Bush at age 12 is already an acomplished and award winning artist. By 5th grade he won the Grand prize in a Drug and Alcohol poster contest for Goshen Schools despite competing against the high school. In 2006 and 2007 he won The Bus Saftey Poster contest for all of New York State. Lee comes from a family that has been farming in Orange County for many generations. He uses his farm as inspiration for his countless drawings and paintings.

STRAWBERRY SALAD

1 head iceberg lettuce
1 head Romaine lettuce
1 small red onion, finely diced
1 lb. strawberries, sliced

Dressing
1 c. mayonnaise
1/2 c. sugar
4 TB. white vinegar
2 TB. poppy seeds

"Red Onion" by Leslie Waxtel.

Break lettuces into bite-size pieces and mix first four ingredients. Whisk dressing ingredients. Add dressing right before serving, as salad gets soggy quickly.

HOT ANTIPASTO BREAD
(recipes courtesy of Diane Mileti, Orange Country Planning Department)

2 small onions sliced very thin
1/4 c. olive oil
1 roasted red pepper, chopped
1/4 lb. finely diced salami
8 slices finely shredded prosciutto
1-1/2 c. shredded mozzarella
5 drained and chopped pepperoncini
1/2 tsp. oregano
4 tsp. red wine vinegar
small can sliced black olives
1 loaf Italian bread, sliced

Saute the onion in oil until soft. Stir in red pepper, salami, prosciutto, mozzarella, pepperoncini, oregano, vinegar, and olives. Spread on slices of Italian bread. Bake at 450 degrees for 5 minutes or until bubbly. Serve warm.

Leslie Waxtel is a painter, working in oil and watercolor. Her colorful landscapes, buildings and nature studies have been exhibited in numerous national and regional shows. She has been a demonstrating artist for the Wallkill River School and resides in Montgomery, NY.

Bounty Cookbook

FRIED GREEN TOMATOES
(courtesy of Susan Cayea, Director Orange County Tourism)

4 large green tomatoes
1/2 cup buttermilk
2 c. corn flour or fine corn meal
2 tablespoon Kosher salt
2 teaspoon pepper
Frying oil

Slice tomatoes into 1/2" slices. Soak in the buttermilk for 5 min. Combine corn meal/flour with salt and pepper. Shake buttermilk off each slice and coat with corn meal mixture. Shake off excess. Bring 2" of oil to 325 degrees. Fry 2 to 3 min. on each side. Drain on paper towels before serving. I place newspaper under the toweling to absorb even more.

HONEY APPLESAUCE
(courtesy of Gerald N. Jacobowitz)

15 apples, divided equally among any three varieties (Macs, Delicious, Jonagold, Matsui, Cortlands, Macom).
10 oz. apple cider (juice as lesser alternate)
4 ozs. honey
2 TB. lemon juice
3 TB. ground cinnamon
1 tsp. ground nutmeg

Peel, core and segment apples into 8 pieces. Rinse in colander. Place in 6 quart sauce pan over medium heat. Add remaining ingredients. Stir after apples start to soften as needed to be mashed. Use potato masher for chunky texture; food processor for finer sauce. Add more honey or cinnamon to taste.

The apple cider and honey ideas are compliments of Mrs. Mark Roe, Roe Orchards, Chester NY.

GRILLED RATATOUILLE
(courtesy of Mary Mugele Sealfon)

2 medium summer squash
   (preferably 1 green and 1 yellow)
1 medium eggplant
1 medium or large onion
1 small bell pepper
1 large tomato chopped
1 clove minced garlic
2 TB. chopped fresh basil
2 TB. olive oil
1 TB. balsamic vinegar
Salt and pepper to taste

Slice squash (lengthwise), eggplant, onion and pepper 1/2"thick.

"Eggplants" by Michelle Filer

Toss them with the olive oil and salt and pepper.
Grill vegetables until they begin to be soft and
grill marks show.
Chop-up the grilled vegetables (no larger than 1") and add to a
 large bowl in which you have mixed the vinegar, garlic, tomato, basil, salt and
pepper. Mix everything together. Serve warm on lettuce with slices of mozzarella on
top or as a side dish, cold or warm. You might also mix in chopped-up protein, such
as tofu, grilled tuna or chicken. Yields 4-6 servings.

"Frederick Franck was a long-time Warwick resident and
world-renown artist and author. Best known for his work
The Zen of Seeing (1973), Franck authored more than
30 book in his 96 year lifespan."

Michelle Filer is a mother first and a painter when her daughters will allow. She lives in Pine Bush with her husband on a farm. Her paintings of the eggs, pumpkin patch and eggplant were for water color spot illustrations

Bounty Cookbook

ITALIAN PASTA SALAD
(courtesy of Diane Mileti, Orange County Planning Department)

1 lb. Rotini pasta (cooked)
3/4 c. olive oil
1/2 c. red or white wine vinegar
1/4 c. sugar
1 TB. dried oregano
1 tsp. salt
1/2 tsp. ground black pepper

2 c. finely diced peppers red and green
1-1/2 c. finely diced onion
2 c. diced ripe tomato
1/4 lb. diced mozzarella
1/4 lb. diced provolone
2 cans chick peas, rinsed
small can or fresh sliced black olives

Cook pasta, rinse with cold water. Whisk together oil, vinegar, sugar and seasonings. Chop peppers, onions, tomato and cheeses. In large bowl, combine pasta and the rest of the ingredients. Make sure pasta is cool before adding cheeses. Toss with dressing. Cover and refrigerate. Toss before serving.

"Warwick artist Daniel Mack makes rustic furniture from sticks and branches, but also organizes huge gatherings in other parts of the country called "Woodlander's Gatherings" attracting scores of people to the beauty of working with natural materials."

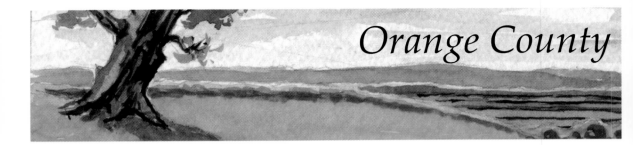

Hoeffner Farm-Montgomery
Farmstand on Route 211 by Orange
County Airport; June-Oct.

"Hoeffner Market Stand", by Lisa O'Gorman Hofsommer

SUMMER SQUASH MEDLEY
(courtesy of Frank and Jane Hoeffner)

4 ears corn cut off the cob
1 lb. zucchini and yellow squash cut
    in 1" slices
3 peeled tomatoes cut in squares
1 onion chopped
2 oz. butter

Mix first three ingredients in a bowl.
In a casserole mix onion with butter. Simmer until onion is yellow. Add corn,
squash and tomato. Season with salt, pepper and fresh basil to taste. Cover and
simmer for 45 minutes. Yield 4 servings

*Montgomery resident Howard Garrett is known
for bringing free Chamber Music Concerts to the public,
but is also a wonderful musician in his own right.
He has two cd's to his credit, and is an
organ grinder, singer, and orchestrion player
among other talents.*

Lisa O'Gorman-Hofsommer, Born & raised in Yonkers, N.Y. Moved to Hudson Valley in 1990. Has been painting in pastels since then and has a strong desire to paint wildlife & landscapes. Created a Pet Portraits business. <Petportraitsnmore.com>. Has been painting with the WRS for four years.She is also am a volunteer sitter for future service dogs.

Bounty Cookbook

ZUCCHINI LASAGNA
(courtesy of Shawn Dell Joyce)

Can be cooked in a solar oven
A variation of a verbal recipe given to me
by Maureen Drury of Walden. Good recipe
for a hearty main course in late summer.

1 HUGE zucchini or two medium squash
or several Patty Pan squash (whatever's
available)

"Hodgson's Farm" by Shawn Dell Joyce

2 fresh eggs
1/4 c. milk
1/2 c. bread crumbs
1 jar Marinara Sauce or homemade sauce
1 lb grated mozzarella or sliced provolone

Slice the squash into long thin strips. Whisk egg and milk for a batter, put bread crumbs in a dish. Dredge each slice in egg/milk mixture, then breadcrumbs. Lightly fry the strips in olive oil. Layer strips of zucchini in a baking dish like you would cooked noodles. Layer marinara sauce on top of the zucchini, then cheese on top of the marinara until the baking dish is filled. Cover lightly with foil and bake in a conventional oven at 350 degrees or a solar oven for four hours. Yields 6-8 servings.

"Walden resident and Hudson Valley Conservancy director Samuel Wright was the voice of Sebastian the Crab on Disney's "The Little Mermaid," and "The Lion King" on Broadway."

Shawn Dell Joyce is a sustainable artist and activist, founder of the Wallkill River School, and writes a syndicated weekly column called "Sustainable Living" in the Sunday Times Herald Record. She has works in major museum collections, and private collections around the world. www.WallkillRiverSchool.com

RIVERA'S RUB
(courtesy of Orange County Tourism)

1 cup garlic cloves
1/4 cup salt
1 tablespoon oregano
2 tablespoon black pepper (freshly crushed)
2 tablespoon extra virgin olive oil

"Peppers", by Susan Miller, (Pastel)

Process all ingredients through food processor resulting in a paste mix. Use Rivera's Rub to season beef, pork, chicken or fish, along with any dishes that call for seasoning. It's also a key ingredient to Pico de Gallo salsa. Yield 2 servings

PICO DE GALLO SALSA
(courtesy of Orange County Tourism)

1 cup cilantro (finely chopped)
1 red pepper
1 Italian green pepper
1 hot pepper
4 large tomatoes
1 large Vidalia onion
3 tablespoon lime juice
3 tablespoon extra virgin olive oil
6 cloves garlic, minced
salt, pepper, oregano to taste

Mix all ingredients. Serve with sliced cucumbers or taco chips. Yield 4-6 servings

Susan Miller received an M.F.A. in drawing and painting from the University of North Texas in 1992 and a B.F.A in painting from SUNY New Paltz in 1988. Miiller paintings explore the subject of artistic transformation and ways of making an age old painting tradition fresh and original.

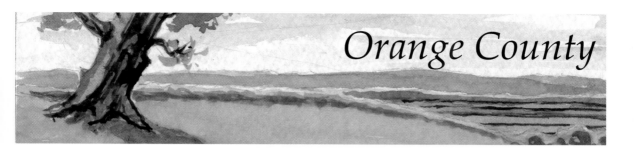

Orange County

Foraging

Orange County is a wonderful place to forage for wild foods. Many Native American tribes like the Lenape once sustained themselves on this fertile soil. Here are a few items you can forage from most back yards and parks and what you can do with them: Burdock is a pesky plant that can be found on most farms.

"Gestation" by Leslie Waxtel

It has burrs that stick to animal fur, and broad fuzzy leaves that form rosettes in the spring. The Japanese use Burdock roots (called Gobo) as a dietary starch staple. It is a great liver cleanser.

JAPANESE SWEET & SOUR GOBO
Based on a recipe by Susan Weed in Wise Woman Herbal

4 Med. Burdock Roots (these take some work to uproot)
2 Tbsp. Tamari
2 Tbsp. Local Honey
2 Tbsp. Vinegar
4 oz. water (1/4 C.)
2 Tbs. Sesame Seeds
Cut burdock into thin, diagonal slices, soak and parboil. Drain, add honey, tamari, vinegar and water, simmer 10 more minutes. Put in a serving dish and sprinkle with sesame.

Dandelions are considered a pest to most homeowners, but in some "old world" countries they are a gift. All parts of the plant are useful and edible, and they are plentiful doe three seasons. The roots make a wonderful alternative to coffee, the greens are great in a salad in early Spring, or sautéed in Summer, and the flowers make wonderful fritters before going to seed.

Leslie Waxtel is a painter, working in oil and watercolor. Her colorful landscapes, buildings and nature studies have been exhibited in numerous national and regional shows. She has been a demonstrating artist for the Wallkill River School and resides in Montgomery, NY.

Bounty Cookbook

Dandelion Fritters
Based on a recipe by Susan Weed in Wise Woman Herbal

1 C. Yellow Dandelion Flowerheads
1 C. Whole Wheat Flour
Pinch of Salt
Fresh Local Egg
1/2 C. Milk (water can be substituted)
2 Tbsp. Olive Oil • Butter • Local Honey

Combine dry ingredients in a medium bowl. Beat egg with oil and milk. Combine with dry ingredients. Pull the yellow petals off the green stems and compost the stems. Fold the yellow petals into the batter. Drop by large spoonfuls onto a greased griddle or large cast iron skillet. Cook like pancakes, turning once. Serve hot with butter and honey.

Foraging for your salad can be a fun dinner party event if you live next to the woods in Orange County. Give guests a pair of scissors and a bowl, make sure they know the difference between poison ivy and violets. Suggest they find the following:
- Chickweed has a lemony flavor and can be found in late spring or early summer filling almost every empty planter or sidewalk crack.
- Violets are precious little purple flowers that are edible and have edible heart-shaped leaves.
- Gooseberries and black caps are tart and delicious, and can be found on prickly shrubs in July.
- dandelion leaves are best picked before the flower buds and blooms.
- Spring onions can be found as slivers of green in early spring, then occasionally through the summer.

Balsamic Vinaigrette to top the salads:
1/2C. Virgin Olive Oil
1/4 C. Balsamic Vinaigrette
1/4 Tsp. Dry Mustard Powder
2 Tbsp. Local Honey
2 Tbsp. Chopped Fresh Parsley

Combine all ingredients in a jar with a tight fitting lid and shake well.

Bounty Cookbook

VEGETARIAN CHILI
(courtesy of Gerald N. Jacobowitz)

4 large carrots
4 stalks celery
1 large onion
2 medium green squash
2 medium yellow squash
1/2 tsp. pepper
1 TB. salt
2-3 cans kidney beans
2 cans stewed or diced tomatoes
1 can tomato sauce or half jar spaghetti sauce
2 TB. small capers
8 ozs. red wine
2 TB. sugar
chili powder

"Carrots" by Mary Evelyn Whitehill

Peel and clean carrots and celery. Cut into 3/4" pieces, sauté in olive oil 5-6 minutes. Place in bowl. Peel and cut onion into 3/4" pieces, sauté in olive oil 4-5 minutes. Combine with carrots and celery in a 6 quart sauce pot. Add squash cut into 3/4" pieces, salt and pepper. Saute and stir 3-4 minutes. Stir every 10 minutes. Add sugar. Cook over low-medium heat 30-45 minutes. Stir every 10 minutes. Add chili powder (or hot sauce) to taste.

"Cornwall resident and handsome Irish-Italian actor Armand Assante, got an impressive start to his acting career when he was awarded one of the American Academy of Dramatic Arts' highest honors while still a student."

Mary Evelyn Whitehill has over 27 years of watercolor experience and is a demonstrating artist for the Wallkill River School. She is also the great-granddaughter of Hudson River School artist Thomas Pope. www.mewhitehill.com

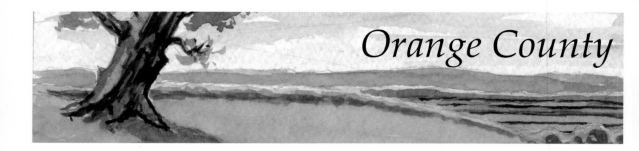

BETTA BRUSCHETTA
(courtesy of Diane Mileti, Orange County
Planning Department)

4 diced tomatoes
1/4 red onion, finely diced
dash of salt
dash of balsamic vinegar
3 basil leaves, finely chopped
1 TB. crushed garlic

3/4 stick butter, softened
2 TB. crushed garlic
16 slices Italian bread
16 slices fresh mozzarella

"Middletown Farmers Market" by
Gloria Detore Mackie

Mix tomatoes, onion, salt, vinegar, basil and 1
tablespoon garlic. Let marinate one hour or more. Mix butter and remaining 2 tablespoons crushed garlic. Spread on Italian bread. Bake at 450 degrees for 5 minutes
(until slightly golden). Top each slice of bread with approximately 1 heaping tablespoon of tomato mixture. Place a slice of mozzarella on top and bake 5 minutes or
until cheese is melted.

*"World-class Shakespearian actor and New Windsor
resident, Jack Aranson was recently awarded an
honorary degree of Doctor of Humane Letters from
Mount Saint Mary College in Newburgh, New York."*

Gloria Detore Mackie is a licensed social worker who practices in Goshen. She is the creator of "Art for Earth;" a nonprofit cultural
consciousness-raising event series combining dance, visual arts and environmental speakers.

Bounty Cookbook

PASTA AND BEAN SALAD
(courtesy of Pat Morgan)

1/2 box ditalini pasta
1 can garbanzo beans, drained
2 stalks scallions, sliced (the bulb and only a little green)
2 tomatoes quartered
1/4 c. chopped basil
2 TB. extra virgin olive oil
2 TB. fresh lemon juice
1/2 TB. mustard
salt and pepper to taste
1/2 c. walnuts, broken by hand (optional)

Cook pasta according to directions. Combine remaining ingredients in a mixing bowl. When pasta is done, drain and add to bowl, toss to mix. Let stand 3-5 minutes and serve.

Note: Low fat or light mayonnaise may be used instead of olive oil and lemon juice.

CORN CHOWDER
(courtesy of Evelyn Johansen)

1 tsp. olive oil
1 medium onion
6 c. corn kernels
3 c. vegetable broth
1/2 c. bell pepper [red or green work equally well]
1/2 tsp. each fresh chopped rosemary and thyme
1/8 tsp. black pepper
Salt to taste

Heat oil in medium sauce pan. Add onion and sauté until translucent. Add 4 cups of corn and cook for 5 more minutes until slightly softened. Add 2 cups broth and simmer for 20 minutes. Puree in blender or food processor. Return to pan. Add bell pepper, herbs, black pepper salt, remaining corn and broth. Stir and cook over medium heat for another 10 minutes. Yields 4 servings.

Farmers' Markets in Orange County
Courtesy of Orange County Tourism
www.OrangeCountyTourism.org
(845) 291-2136

Florida Farmers' Market Rt. 17A, across from Big V Shoprite HQ,
       Tuesday 10am - 4:30pm June 19 - October 9, 641-4482

Goshen Farmers' Market Village Square - Intersection of Main & Church Sts.
       Friday 10am - 5pm May 18 - October 26, 294-7741

Middletown Farmers' Market Erie Way from Grove St. to Cottage St.
       Saturday 8am - 1pm, June 16 - October 27, 343-8075

Monroe Farmers' Market Museum Village Parking lot, 1010 Rt. 17 M,
       Wednesday 9am - 3pm, June 22 - October 25, 344-1234

Newburgh/Downing Park Farmers' Market In Downing Park in Newburgh, near the corner of South St. (NYS Rt. 52) & Robinson Ave. (Rt. 9W)
       Friday 10 AM - 5 PM, July 13 - October 26, 565-5559

Pine Bush Farmers' Market Parking lot at New & Depot Sts.
       Saturday 9am - 2pm, June 9 - October 20 , 744-6763

Tri State Farmers' Market Parking lot bet. Ball St. & Front St. in Port Jervis
       Saturday 8am - 2pm June 30 - October 27, 856-6694

Tuxedo Farmers' Market 240 Rt. 17 N. , Tuxedo Train Station
       Saturday 9am - 2pm, June 16 - October 27, 915-4058 ext.523

Walden Village Square Farmers' Market Fireman's Square next to Municipal Square in front of Library & Village Square
       Thursday 12 Noon - 4 PM June 28 - October 25, 294-5557

Warwick Valley Farmers' Market, South St. parking lot, off Main St.,
       Sunday 9am - 2pm, May 20 - October 28, 987-9990

West Point/Town of Highlands Farmers' Market Municipal lot, Main Street near Visitors Ctr.
       Sunday 9am - 2:30pm June 24 – October28, 446-2459

Orange County Bounty Cookbook

Fall

(October, November, December)

What's in season?

Fruits

Apples

Grapes (from September)

Pears (until Mid October)

Plums (until Mid October)

Raspberries (October)

Vegetables

Beans (until Mid October)

Beets (through November)

Broccoli (through October)

Cabbage

Carrots

Cauliflower

Celery (until Mid November)

Corn (until Mid October)

Cucumbers (until Mid October)

Eggplant (until Mid October)

Herbs (Cilantro, Parsley, Rosemary, Thyme)

Lettuces (until Mid October)

Onions (through October)

Peppers (until Mid October)

Potatoes (until Mid October)

Pumpkins (Mid September-October)

Radishes (until Mid November)

Spinach (until Mid October)

Winter Squash (until Mid November)

Tomatoes (until Mid October)

Turnips (until Mid November)

Meats

Chicken, Turkey, Pheasant

Pork, Beef, Venison, Goat

Honey

Eggs

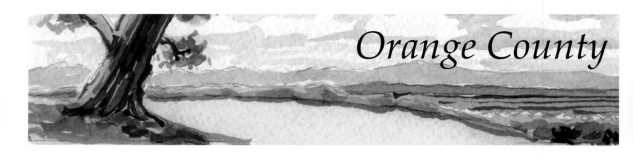

YOU CAN, CAN!

In earlier days, canning was the only economical method for preserving wholesome food for the winter months. With the recent developments in food distribution and technology, canning is not as popular as it once was. With the recent move toward organic and unconventional farming and gardening, home canning could become an economical solution for healthier fruits and vegetables during the winter months.

"Tomatoes", by Alix Travis.

Today, home canning is safe and as easy as cooking a meal, providing proper methods are followed. You need only invest in canning jars, rings and caps and a pressure canner.

I recommend pressure canning, as it is more efficient in use of energy and water.

Many people have traded in their canning jars for freezer containers. A plus for canning is that there are some foods that are much better canned than frozen. Sauerkraut doesn't freeze well at all; it loses its crispiness. The same goes for most pickled foods. Pears get too soft when frozen but not when they are canned. And canned beets are much preferred to frozen ones.

I prefer freezer jams and jellies but find they take up too much space and break easily. Therefore I seal them using the pressure canner. They make wonderful gifts.

If you have never done any home canning please contact: Cornell Cooperative Extension of Orange County. **Phone: 845-344-1234. Fax, 845-343-7471**, and request information and resources.

Lois Ford Schwab was the "home economist" at Lloyds in Middletown, and had a weekly nutritional column in the Times Herald Record, until becoming the administrator for the Orange County Office of the Aging.

When shorter days are noticeable and the burning bush starts to look like red flames, the last of the year's pickle making is at hand. Finally, the green tomatoes can be picked to make green tomato pickles and packed to ripen for the fall feasts. This is an old Ford family recipe.

Green Tomato Pickles

2 quarts green tomatoes, sliced 3/8 inch thick
3 small onions, sliced 1/4 inch thick.
1 large red pepper, chopped.
1/3 cup salt

2 cups cider vinegar
2/3 cup brown sugar
1 cup white sugar
1 1/2 teaspoons celery seed
1 1/2 teaspoons whole cloves
1 1/2 teaspoons mustard seed
1 small stick cinnamon

Soak the tomatoes, onions and pepper sprinkled with 1/3 cup salt for 2 hours.

Tie the spices in a cheese cloth bag or tea caddy. Heat the vinegar, sugars and spices to a boil and let simmer until slightly thickened; add the drained vegetables; bring slowly to a boil. Simmer gently 15 to 20 minutes, stirring gently with a wooden spoon. Pack into hot sterilized jars. Be sure syrup covers vegetables. Leave _ inch space from top of jar. Screw on rings over hot lids tightly. Process in boiling water bath 15 minutes. Remove jars to cool.

Alix Hallman-Travis is an award-winning watercolorist who believes in painting every day, from life, and all at once. She is a demonstrating artist for the Wallkill River School, and is represented by several galleries including the Wallkill River Gallery.

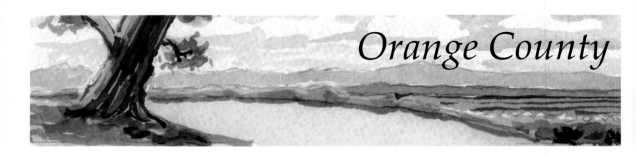

"Preserving the Harvest"
Dehydrating by Shawn Dell Joyce

My favorite preservation method is dehydrating fresh produce. You don't use up all your freezer space, and there's little chance of improper processing. Also, nothing beats the intensified flavor of a sundried tomato in mid winter. I was fortunate enough to snag a used dehydrator from a friend for free. If you can't find one at a yard sale, try using clean window screens for a low-tech version. Hot dry summer days are perfect for rooftop dehydrating. To process, make sure you wash the tomatoes well, and lay them out to dry on a dishtowel. In the meantime, set up your dehydrator or screens. I spray each tray with a nonstick cooking spray to keep dehydrated produce from sticking. This is essential if you are using window screens. Quarter tomatoes, and slide your thumb along the inside to remove the pulp. Lay tomato quarters evenly spaced on the trays so air will circulate around them. When one tray is filled, lightly salt the tomatoes with sea salt. Fill up all the trays, and then drape a dishtowel over the top tray (or sandwich another screen on top) to keep gnats away.

My dehydrator uses a tiny fan and very little electricity, so I fill it up before bed, and leave it on all night. In the morning, I take out the first few trays and store the crispy dried tomatoes in a jar or waxed paper bag in the pantry. If you like your tomatoes a little softer, take the next few trays out as well. I am leery of soft dried tomatoes spoiling, so I store the softer ones in the freezer in a small container. I have a Greek friend who stores soft dried tomatoes in a jar with garlic cloves and olive oil in the refrigerator.

Toward the end of August, I keep the dehydrator fully loaded and running night and day. It becomes a ritual to gut tomatoes, and trade out the shriveled little morsels for fleshy red wedges. It's very little work and takes about as much time as a phone call to a friend. You also have the added benefit of a warm tomato smell infusing your home.

Tomatoes are not the only fresh produce that is exceptionally yummy in its dried form. Zucchini, believe it or not, is exquisite when crisped in a dehydrator. Peaches make a wonderful dried fruit snack. Strawberries, blueberries and raspberries are also good, but I puree them in a blender and spread the pulp on waxed paper in the dehydrator tray. A few things that flopped were green beans, corn, bell peppers and cucumbers. A big hit from the dehydrator was homemade organic, pasture-raised beef jerky. It's an expensive treat, but much better for you and the environment than its store-bought counterpart.

Bounty Cookbook

"Preserving the Harvest" - Freezing Tips
By Jim Hyland, President - Winter Sun Farms

As is typical of many Community Supported Agriculture (C.S.A.) members I found myself surrounded by a lot of beautiful produce. Unfortunately there was no way my family could eat it all before it went bad. In a desperate pinch I hit the search key on the computer and found the easiest and fastest way to preserve: freezing.

The basics are: Clean / Blanche / Ice Bath / Drain / Package / Freeze

I reached for my towering pile of fall greens and started to go. I washed them, blanched them for a minute, plunged them into an ice-bath for minute, drained them, put them into a freezer bag, and into the freezer. I had saved my greens, but the real pay-off came that winter. On a cold December day I pulled a bag of greens out, and added them to a stew of beans I was making. I could taste the flavor of summer and felt I could even taste the vitamins themselves...delicious.

Tips:
- Only use the best. If you start with bad produce, you will get bad frozen produce.
- Blanche times vary for all produce, check before starting. (Some things like peppers and berries don't need to be blanched, just cleaned and frozen.)
- The ice-bath stops the cooking so keep it real cold and add ice as you go.
- Drain well or use a salad spinner. Less moisture = Less ice crystals
- Plastic bags are great, but containers are good too. Make sure to leave head space in containers
- Back of freezer freezes quicker. Quicker freeze = Better product
- Vegetables like winter squash, tomatoes, and berries can be cooked down into a puree before freezing.

Blanching times for specific vegetables:

Peppers	0 minutes	Greens	1 minute	Berries	0 minutes
Corn	2 minutes	Squash	3 minutes	Beans	3 minutes

By Jim Hyland, President - Winter Sun Farms
195 Huguenot Street, New Paltz, NY 12561 845-255-1699 www.WinterSunFarms.com

Soons Orchard

23 Soons Circle,
New Hampton, NY
(845) 374-5471
www.soonsorchards.com

"Soons Orchards" by Marge Morales

It's 1910, and William Soons is an electrical engineer living and working in New York City. Enough comes to be enough, and Soons sets out to try his luck at dairy farming. He and his family move north, and Soons begins doing something he's always loved - planting trees.

He plants hardwoods. He plants apple trees. He plants pear trees and he plants peach trees.

In time, one of the Soons' sons, Sinclair, discovers that he has ideas for expansion. He begins wholesaling apples, and he expands the dairy.

By the 1930's, he's married Helen and taken over farm operations. Soons (known at the time as Orchard Hill) buys its first tractor in1939.

Sinclair and Helen have children, and the children turn their hearts, ideas and educations back into the soil of the farm. The youngest, Arthur, works with his wife Sandy to grow Soons. Jeffrey, who is also an attorney, takes over orchard and farm operations. Laura and her husband Scott found Scotty's Country Kitchen, which celebrates 20 years this year . The youngest, Sharon, spends 10 years in the city, working in the nonprofit world, before returning to the farm and starting her own business, Streamline U., a professional organizing business for home or work.

There are lots of great things about being a farmer, the Soons say. And one of the best, Art Soons says, is "zero commute!"

Eating locally, Sandy Soons says, is vital. It preserves farms and open spaces. "Plus, it just tastes better." Sandy's concern for the environment extends beyond the farm; among other things, she serves as treasurer for Orange Environment.

Bounty Cookbook

APPLE TART
(courtesy of Sandy Soons, Soons Orchards)

8 c. peeled, sliced cooking apples (2-3 lbs. Idareds, Winesaps)
1 c. sugar
1 tsp. cinnamon
2 tsp. lemon juice
1 tsp. lemon peel (yellow part only)
2 tsp. cornstarch
3-4 TB. chopped nuts
3-4 TB. raisins
1 pie crust cut in strips
1 egg + one tsp. water

Sprinkle sliced apples with lemon juice and lemon peel. Mix sugar, cinnamon, and cornstarch in a jar. Add nuts, raisins, and sugar mixture to apples—mix well. Arrange in 8"x8"x2" baking dish. Slice pie crust into strips and arrange on top of mixture—brush with egg if desired. Cook at 400 for 40-60 minutes until top is brown and apples are tender. Yield 6 servings

"Orange County ranks second in the state for vegetable production, and third for nurseries and greenhouses."

What Sandy would like her Orange County neighbors to know is simple and to the point.

"We are honest," she says. "And we care."

Soons's New Hampton store is open close to year-round. It sells fresh produce and much more, even in the winter.

Marge Morales of Rock Tavern sees herself as a modern-day storyteller, using paint as her medium. In oils and watercolors, Marge offers more than images; her art tells stories that touch the heart and the soul.

Sycamore Farms
Wallkill, NY
(845) 692-2684
www.SycamoreFarmsny.com

"Pumpkin Pickers" (Sycamore Farms), by Shawn Dell Joyce, (Pastel 2006) collection of the farmers Sue & Henry Smith.

Sycamore Farms is on Route 211 just outside Montgomery past Bull Road. You may recognize it by the stately sycamore in the front yard of the picturesque farm house, or the grey barn across the street. If you're lucky enough to be a friend of the Smith's, you know what delicious sweet corn they grow. The Smith family has owned this farm since 1979, and has been a working farm since 1981. Like most of our farms, the Smith family sells most of the produce to the green markets. Recently, Sue Smith has decided to open her family's farm to the public as a community supported agriculture (C.S.A.) project. This means that all of us can enjoy fresh, locally grown vegetables every week from the farm.

Sycamore Farms started with a dream, as a young couple from Rockland County, landed here and sank roots into Orange County's fertile soil. Four children were born to Sue and Henry Smith, three daughters; Laurie, Tammy, and Krista, and one son; Kevin. Sycamore Farms, along with a neighboring property, is being considered for a Farmland Preservation Grant. If the farm is preserved, it will lessen the heavy tax burden the Smiths shoulder every year.

"Whenever we had extra money," says Henry, "we bought more land." The farm's acreage has increased three-fold since Henry Smith purchased it in 1979. "This farm is our retirement," notes Henry, who looks far from being ready to retire. This is a good thing because Kevin would have a lot of work for one pair of hands to support both households.

"Orange County has over 52 farms that retail edibles directly to Orange County residents."

KOHLRABI COLESLAW
(courtesy of Sycamore Farms)

1 pound kohlrabi (3-4) peeled and cut into 1/4 inch strips
1 Medium carrot cut into 1/8 inch strips
1 tbs. minced chives
1 tbs lemon juice
1 tbs butter melted
2 tsp honey
1/4 tsp grated lemon peel
1/8 tsp pepper
4 lemon slices

In large skillet bring 1 inch of water, kohlrabi and carrot to a boil. Reduce heat, cover and simmer for 6-10 minutes or until crisp-tender.

In a small bowl, combine the chives, lemon juice, buter, honey, lemon peel and pepper: mix well. Drain vegetables and transfer to a serving bowl. Add honey butter and toss to coat. Garnish with lemon slices. Yield 4 servings

*"Just under Interstate Route 84 bridge
in Port Jervis, at the junction of the
Neversink and Delaware Rivers is the "Tri-State Rock."
You can stand on this rock and be in three states at once ,
as it is officially recognized as the place where
New York, New Jersey and Pennsylvania meet."*

Shawn Dell Joyce is a sustainable artist and activist, founder of the Wallkill River School, and writes a syndicated weekly column called "Sustainable Living" in the Sunday Times Herald Record. She has works in major museum collections, and private collections around the world. www.WallkillRiverSchool.com

Walnut Grove LLC
285 Youngblood Road
Montgomery NY 12549
Farm Store Open June-Dec.
Hours: Wed-Fri 3-5pm
Sat 8am-3pm
 www.WalnutGroveFarms.net
Ned Roebuck 845 313 4855

"Walnut Grove Famstand" by Shawn Dell Joyce, (Pastel 2006)

The Roebuck family has farmed on Youngblood Road in the Town of Crawford for more than 50 years. The focus of the farm during this time has ranged from a conventional dairy herd, a commercial poultry farm, to an organic farm raising Belted Galloway beef cows as well as vegetables. In the 1970's the dairy herd and the poultry operation were sold and the land was used to make hay for local farmers. There have been no chemicals used on any of the acreage since the sale of the conventional farms. In 2003, Walnut Grove LLC was created with the needs of today's consumers in mind; natural, without chemicals or additives. Today, the farm is Certified Organic and is run by brother and sister team Ned and Holly Roebuck. The Roebuck family operates a small farm store that is open to the public from 3-5pm Mon-Fri. and sells homemade breads, jams, pastured beef, pork and eggs, and delicious pies. The vegetables grown on the farm are reserved for C.S.A. customers (you pay a lump sum for a weekly share of the harvest). You can often find fresh fruit and dairy products sold in the Walnut Grove Farm Store from other local farms.

"Artifacts dating before the Ice Age (12,000 years ago) were found at the Town Park at Benedict Farm in Montgomery along the Wallkill River, making it one of the longest populated areas in Orange County."

SPICY SAUSAGE STUFFED ZUCCHINI SHELLS
(courtesy of Valerie Roebuck, Walnut Grove)

Serving size = 2 "shells" or 1/2 of a zucchini.
3 med.-to-large zucchini
4-6 hot Italian sausage links removed from casings (venison blend is excellent),
1/2 red pepper, finely chopped
1 onion, chopped
4 cloves garlic, finely chopped
Olive oil
Oregano, about 1/2 TB.
Fine corn meal
Mozzarella cheese, grated

Cut zucchini in half length-wise and in half cross-wise. Scoop out pulp so zucchini shells are about _-1/2" thick. If the seeds are tough then discard. Otherwise, chop the zucchini pulp and set aside. In large pot, bring about 2" of water to boil. Add zucchini shells, cover, and cook for 7 minutes. Drain immediately and cool.

In the meantime, in a large nonstick skillet, add approx. 2 TB. olive oil and heat on medium. Add garlic, onion, pepper. Stir until coated with oil. Add reserved zucchini pulp and sausage, carefully breaking up the sausage into smaller pieces. Saute all for approximately 8 minutes, or until sausage is completely cooked and vegetables are tender. Add the oregano and stir. There should be liquid in the pan. Add approximately 2 TB. fine cornmeal and mix thoroughly; if still too wet, add a little more cornmeal. Combine. Remove from heat.

Heat oven to 375. Place the shells face up in an ovenproof casserole dish. Fill each shell with the meat and vegetable mixture. Load 'em up! Sprinkle shredded mozzarella cheese atop each one and bake in a preheated oven for approximately 20-25 minutes. Yield 6 servings

Shawn Dell Joyce is a sustainable artist and activist, founder of the Wallkill River School, and writes a syndicated weekly column called "Sustainable Living" in the Sunday Times Herald Record. She has works in major museum collections, and private collections around the world. www.WallkillRiverSchool.com

Abundant Life Farm
168 Prospect Road
Middletown
(845) 692-3550

When Linda Borghi was 7, she lived near Rome.
Her dad, an art dealer, would often leave Linda and
her brother with their grandmother for the weekends. Though neither child spoke Italian, they all
managed to understand each other.

"Abundant Life Farm", by Gloria Detore Mackie

Hungry? the grandmother would ask. Linda would
nod, and grandmother would tell her to go into the yard and catch a chicken. Linda soon
found it was a harder task than it seemed. Her grandmother came out and barely looked
down as, Linda says, she "gracefully caught our supper."

Over a bowl of the best chicken soup she'd ever tasted, Linda decided she wanted to be just
like her little Italian grandmother.

Linda enjoys her work, especially the connection it gives her to life itself. She's in awe of
the creative process and loves being a part ofit.

The food you get from the local farm is fresh, she says, "the way ahealthy body needs it to
be." And in the process of getting that fresh food, intimate relationships develop between the
farmer and the consumer. As the buyer gets to know the farmer, the buyer realizes what it
takes to bring a meal to the table. "Then and only then," she says, "will food be honored as a
gift and the farmer as the giver of that gift."

Without the farmer, Linda says, life on Earth could not continue."Man, despite his artistic
pretensions, his sophistication and his many accomlishments, owes his existence to a 6-inch
layer of topsoil and the fact that it rains."

Linda's grandmother died in the late 1980s, when Linda was farming on Block Island. And
Linda knows, to this day, that her grandmother was proud of her.

BOUNTIFUL BRUSSEL SPROUTS
(courtesy of Linda Borghi)

5 lbs. brussel sprouts
6 large onions
Dijon mustard

Quarter and steam the brussel sprouts and set aside. Quarter the onions and place them in a shallow pan with water and place in a 250 degree oven for about 2 hours, replacing the water until the onions have released all of their wonderful onion sugar. When the onions are goopy enough, mix with the brussel sprouts and Dijon mustard. Yield A large group

"Still Life with Onion," by Bob Grawi

Gloria Detore Mackie is a licensed social worker who practices in Goshen. She is the creator of "Art for Earth;" a nonprofit cultural consciousness-raising event series combining dance, visual arts and environmental speakers.

Bob Grawi, the inventor of the Gravikord, is an artist and musician based in Florida, New York.

Iron Forge Inn
Bellvale, NY 10912
845-986-3411
www.ironforgeinn.com

The Iron Forge Inn in Warwick has been an independent, family-owned restaurant for more than 55 years. In a Revolutionary-era home, built in 1760 at the foot of Mount Peter, the inn is also the site of a historic forge. Head chef Erik Johansen, a graduate of the Culinary Institute of America, emphasizes local ingredients and seasonal availability in his menus.

"Iron Forge Inn", by Bruce Thorne.

"Being a chef," he says, "puts me in touch one of mankind's most basic needs – to eat. But it goes beyond that. Growing up, my parents always had dinner on the table for us. It wasn't just about the food, it was also the communal experience of being a family. I want people to sit and eat with us and create memories that will last long after they leave. Eating, laughing, sitting together with those that we care for– that's what I hope to provide for our guests."

The Iron Forge Inn serves two menus. The pub-style menu served in the Tap Room, is popular with the local clientele, Johansen says. Above the Tap Room are more formal dining rooms which feature a more formal menu, focusing on local seasonal products.

"The food we serve is focused on quality," he says. Creativity is at play for Johansen in building the menu as well as cooking the dishes. He gets ideas and inspiration from the availability of materials, and also from his staff.

"Eating locally just tastes better," he says. "It supports the local economy and benefits the environment. Eating with a 'sense of place' makes the meal that much more memorable. Great food comes from people, it should not be reduced to a UPC code hidden in a warehouse 3,000 miles away."

Bruce Thorne-His style has been compared to Van Gogh for his rich color, thick impasto paint technique and his passion for painting.

PINE ISLAND ONION BREAD PUDDING
(courtesy of The Iron Forge Inn)
FOR THE ONION CUSTARD-
5 whole onions, unpeeled (we use local Pine Island onions) • 2 c. heavy cream
2 c. whole milk • 2 TB. salt • 1 bay leaf • 4 thyme sprigs
10 whole black peppercorns • 7 egg yolks • 2 whole eggs • 1 TB. lemon juice
Preheat oven to 350 degrees. Wrap the onions individually in aluminum foil and bake until the centers are very soft. About 1.5 minutes. Don't even think about peeling them right out of the oven – just walk away. The onions are now steaming little bombs just waiting to burn you. Let the onions cool before peeling. Gather and measured the ingredients for the custard. The bay leaf, thyme and black peppercorn are to be wrapped in cheesecloth and tied with butchers twine to make a sachet. Peel the onions and cut them into large chunks. Puree in a blender or food processor until smooth.

In a 2 quart sauce pot, combine the roasted onion puree, cream, milk, 1 tablespoon of salt and the herb sachet and bring to a boil. Do not to let the mixture boil over. Reduce the heat to a very low simmer and cook for 15 minutes. Remove from the heat. Mix the remaining 1 tablespoon of salt with the eggs in a stainless steel bowl. Whisk to liquefy the mixture. While stirring with a whisk, slowly drizzle in the hot cream mixture until everything is combined and then strain the mixture back into the stainless steel bowl. Add the lemon juice.

To assemble the Bread Pudding- 9 cups bread, diced _" (chewy French loaves work great) • Onion custard mix • Pan spray as needed
Set the oven to 325 degrees. Using pan spray, lubricate the bottom and sides of a 9"x9" pan. Line the bottom of a pan with parchment paper and spray the paper. Combine the bread and onion custard mix, squeezing the bread to allow the custard to absorb. Let the mixture sit for at least 30 minutes before cooking. Cover with foil. Set the pan with the bread pudding mixture into a roasting pan and place into the oven, pour enough hot water into the roasting pan to come half way up the sides of the bread pudding pan. Bake for 1 to 1.5 hours. The finished mixture should jiggle in one solid mass like a cooked cheesecake or crème brulee. If the center is still "liquidy", the foil may be removed to help with the last few minutes of cooking. The onion bread pudding may be served immediately or cooled and reheated. If serving straight from the oven, the consistency will require a spoon. If it is cooled and reheated the custard can be cut into portion size shapes – simply invert the cold bread pudding onto a cutting board and cut.

Ananda Ashram
Monroe, NY

Ananda Ashram, in
Monroe, was established as
a spiritual retreat center in
1964. Also an educational
center, the Ashram was
founded on the universal
principles of yoga and
Vedanta - a school of
thought within Hinduism
dealing with the nature of reality - and dedicated to East-
West cultural exchange. It was established in 1964 as the country center of the Yoga
Society of New York, Inc.

"Ananda Ashram" by Lita Thorne.

Harve` Moroz, who provided the recipe, loved to cook "because it gives me a chance to
meet new people and do something nice for them. I also like challenges, such as cooking
for people with special diets." And, he adds, it's a wonderful experience to see where the
food comes from.

Moroz believes it's important to support the local community, especially farmers. It is
important to me to support my local community, especially the farmers. In addition, he
enjoys educating people about vegetarian cooking, especially at a fine dining level.

I enjoy educating people about vegetarian cooking, especially at a fine dining level. It is a
joy to show people a healthy, local-food-based way to eat.

"The 30-year battle to preserve Storm King Mountain
became the basis for the U.S. environmental law,
and brought national attention to the highest peak
on the west bank of the Hudson Highlands. "

Bounty Cookbook

GRANDMA DE MARLO'S CARROT DELIGHT
Harve Moroz

4 c. grated carrots
1/4 c. crushed walnuts
1/4 c. chopped cilantro
1/4 c. thinly sliced apples
1/4 c. raisins
3 TB. sugar
3 TB. apple cider vinegar
1/4 c. lime juice
some water

"Carrots" by Pat Morgan.

Combine in a medium bowl: carrots, walnuts, cilantro and apples. In a pot, combine raisins and sugar. Add water, just enough to cover the raisins and bring to a boil. When raisins become soft, add vinegar and lime juice and turn off heat. Pour raisin mixture into carrot mixture, mix and chill. Serve cold.

Ananda Ashram was established as a spiritual retreat center in 1964. I love to cook because it gives me a chance to met new people and do something nice for them. I also like challenges, such as cooking for people with special diets. It is important to me to support my local community, especially the farmers. As a chef, it is a wonderful experience to see exactly where the food is coming from. Yield 6 servings

Lita Thorne-Lita's grandparents' Blackfeet Indian heritage can be felt in her vibrant color palette and simple designs.

Pat Morgan, a watercolor painter, has studied with artists including Richard Ochs, Eli Rosenthal and Mel Stabin. Currently, she is represented by the Wallkill River Gallery. She has received local and regional awards for her work, and enjoys teaching other painters her love of watercolor.

Maggie's in The Alley
39 Main St.
Chester, NY
(845) 469-8272
www.maggiesinthealley.com

"Maggie's in the Alley" by Johanna Kiernan

The building at 39 Main Street that houses Maggie's and Bodles Opera House was built in 1855 as a carriage and sleigh factory by Samuel Hadden. In 1885, he sold to one of his employees, George Brooks, who continued the business, supplying local folks with buggies, wagons and many styles of carriages. With Brooks's death, his son, Clarence, took over the business, bringing it into the 20th century, transferring it from horse to auto industry in 1926. New Chevrolets were sold here, as was gasoline, and auto repairs were done, too.

In 1985, Jarvis Boone bought the building, saved it from demolition, built a stage and brought his vaudeville-style act to Chester. Staffing the restaurant with singing waiters, waitresses and bartenders, they, along with Jarvis, were the show. In 1999, Patricia Mazo, one of Boone's singing waitresses purchased the business and continues the vaudeville/ cabaret show the first and third Saturday nights of each month.

Patricia and her sister Jo Gillman opened Maggie's In The Alley, named for their maternal grandmother Margaret Graham Inman. The interior is constructed from recycled church pews, the ceiling is a reproduction of an original design used in the downtown area and the back bar was recovered from an old bar room in Middletown formerly known as Maggie's, (an unknown fact until recently).

In September 2005, CIA graduate and now Executive Chef James Devaney took over Maggie's menu and brought in a fresh new concept of tapas. Now with an incredible staff, marvelous martinis and an eclectic reasonably priced wine list, it is no wonder that Maggie's In The Alley was voted Number ONE by the Times Herald-Record!

"Philadelphia Brand Cream Cheese was actually invented in Chester in 1872."

Bounty Cookbook

SWEET CORN, CARAMELIZED APPLE AND SAFFRON RISOTTO
(courtesy of Chef James Devaney)

1 tbs. olive oil • 1/2 c. chopped onions • 2 tbs. minced shallots
2 tbs. minced garlic • 2 c. Arborio rice • 1 c. dry white wine

4 c. corn stock, infused with 6 threads of saffron
1 tbs. unsalted butter
2 teas. salt
1 teas. white pepper
1/2 c. chopped green onions
1 c. sweet corn kernels
1 c. lightly caramelized green apples, cut into 1 inch dice
3/4 c. grated Parmesan Reggiano

In a sauté pan, heat the olive oil. When the pan is smoking hot, sauté the onions, shallots and garlic for 1 minute. Using a wooden spoon, stir in the rice and sauté for 1 minute. Stir in wine and reduce till rice is almost dry. Stir in butter and 1/2 cup of the stock at a time until all of the liquid is incorporated, about 3 minutes. Season with salt and pepper. Bring up to boil, reduce heat and simmer about 10 minutes. Fold in the sweet corn and apples to warm. Fold minced chives and cheese and spoon into four bowls.

*Corn stock can be made by boiling 6 corn husks with a bay leaf and garlic for 30 minutes. Use low sodium chicken stock if you wish. Sautee the apples in about 2 tablespoons of melted butter over medium high heat until they have some color but remain firm. Yield 4-6 servings

*"Hambletonian 10; a stallion bred by Jonas Seely Jr.
on his Sugar Loaf farm, is the ancestor of
99% of all harness racing trotters today.."*

Johanna Kiernan - Student of Andre Girard, QCC, Bayside, NY; B.A. Queens College; Masters Program Pratt Institute; Apprentice Modern Art Foundry, LIC, NY & Excalibur Bronze, Brooklyn NY; President of Reilly League of Artists, White Plains, NY; member Wallkill River Painting School, Montgomery, NY.

Scheuermann Farm
Warwick, NY

Bob is the 5th generation working this Warwick farm. The Scheuermanns migrated from Prussia in the 1700's and settled on Little York Rd. Their house was the first constructed in the German settlement. The recent Scheuermanns were married in 1970, and both came from farming families. They raised two children Rod and Erin, and diversified the farm from raising only onions to a wide variety of produce. The farm also changed from wholesale to retail, and added greenhouses to retail fresh flowers. The farm is growing still and opening a retail gift shop.

"Ronnies Field and Barn", by Ronnie Mehrberg Lipitz.

The family affectionately calls their farm; "our slice of heaven," and their customers agree. Lucky people wander through the 5 acres of fresh flowers and relax on the lush lawn to hear a free concert from the Warwick Summer Arts Festival. The farmers are proud of the rich black soil and will give brief history lessons to any who ask. "We take great pride in what we do. We work seven days a week to provide our customers with a variety of fresh vegetables."

"Buying local produce is the only way to eat fresh," says the Scheuermanns. "We do not sell at the farm markets because we want people to come to our beautiful farm. See where your produce is grown and know you are getting a fresh, healthy product. When you buy local, you are supporting a fellow tax payer who in turn gives you safe fresh produce you can count on. Other countries do not have the strict standards for chemical use and food handling that we do. If we do not support our local farms, they will disappear and we will be left with only imported food."

The Scheuermanns say that the "signs are not promising for farmers." Citing the high overhead and slim profits. They claim their produce price has not risen over the past 37 years, while the expenses of running a farm have. "If you think there's gambling in Las Vegas, Try Farming."

TERIYAKI BARBEQUED ONIONS
(courtesy of Scheuermann Farms)

1 medium yellow onion
1 tsp. teriyaki
1 TB. butter
salt and pepper

Peel onion and cut both ends off. Make four or five slices in the top of the onion, making sure not to cut all the way through, so the onion stays in one piece. Set onion on a large piece of foil. Drizzle onion with teriyaki sauce, salt, pepper; place a pat of butter on top and seal the foil tightly. Place on the grill for 20-30 minutes until tender. Yield 2 servings

"Four Onions" by Leslie Waxtel.

"26% of Orange County is open spaces in the form of parks, reservoir lands and nature preserves. This doesn't include farmlands."

Ronnie Mehrberg Lipitz-A Former High School art teacher. Studied art at Adelphi University, Pratt, Parsons, FIT, and SVA. Is currently painting at the Art Student's league and with The Wallkill River School of Painting. She lives in New York City and In Sugarloaf, N.Y.

Leslie Waxtel is a painter, working in oil and watercolor. Her colorful landscapes, buildings and nature studies have been exhibited in numerous national and regional shows. She has been a demonstrating artist for the Wallkill River School and resides in Montgomery, NY.

Roe's Orchards
Chester NY
(845) 469-4724.

Roe's Orchards is a NYS Century Farm,
meaning it has been farmed continuously
by the same family for over 100 years. The
farm is now owned and operated by the 5th
and 6th generation of the Roe family, Mark
Roe and oldest son Tom Roe.

The farm was purchased in 1827 by Mark's
great-great uncle. Like many farms of that
period, the farm consisted of a few cows,
chickens, pigs, and a small orchard. By the
1950's the farm focused on the orchard and
the growing of fruit.

In the 1960's the Roes saw the need to enter
the retail market in a bigger way at their
farm store. They started growing a variety
of vegetables and added a cider mill. The
business grew, with the population, and a
renewed enthusiasm for locally grown fruits and vegetables.

"Roe's Orchards" by Karen Schoonmaker.

The farm store opens in late July with peaches and home grown vegetables. The season
progresses with a good variety of apples, pears, plums, fresh-pressed cider, and homemade
apple pies. The season lasts into the winter.

Grandchildren are often seen helping out at the farm store. Hopefully there will be a 7th
generation operating this Chester family farm.

APPLESAUCE CAKE
(courtesy of Roe's Orchards)

Mix:
1-1/2 c. applesauce (homemade chunky is best)
3/4 c. light brown sugar
1/2 c. canola oil

Sift into large bowl:
1-3/4 c. flour
1 tsp. baking soda
1/2 tsp salt
1 tsp. cinnamon
1/2 tsp. cloves

Add:
3/4 c. raisins
1/2 c. walnuts, chopped

"Cantalope, peaches, and shiro plums from Roe's Orchards", by Lisa Toth.

Add applesauce mixture to bowl and blend well. In a 9" x 13" pan, bake at 350 degrees about 45 minutes – test with toothpick. Butter frosting is nice but cake is delicious sprinkled with powdered sugar.

"Orange County, NY is the first of 8 counties named Orange in the U.S."

Karen Schoonmaker - A landscape and still life painter, karen divides her time between painting and teaching art in the Goshen, NY school district. Exhibiting locally and on Long Island, her work can be seen in print as well as in public and private collections.

Lisa Toth is a painter living in Chester, NY. She is primarily a painter of still lifes of fruit and vegetables from local farms.

Bialas Farms

Goshen Farmers' Market
www.BialasFarms.com

Bialas Farms is a family-run farm that grows over 80 different varieties of vegetables on 55 acres of beautiful muck soil. Their story begins in 1939 with Sophie and Francis Bialas who had farmed for years, not mass quantities, but just enough to get by. It was during the Great Depression that Francis and Sophie purchased a few acres of prized Orange County Black Dirt on Celery Avenue, where Sophie had lived as a young girl. Appropriately, Frank and Sophie started with celery.

"Bialas Farm", by Steve Blumenthal

As the years went by, more acres were added (totaling 55) and more kids were born (6 altogether) and Bialas Farms was in full swing! Everyone helped out, too. Grandma Sophie and Grandpa Francis worked all day with the hired help, and when the kids came home from school they'd go out to work so Babci (Polish for Grandma) could come home and cook dinner for 8 hungry farmers!

Bialas Farms currently has 3 greenhouses in which a vast number of potted herbs and an assortment of baby greens are grown. The farm has done well in the markets, and with each year it has expanded the product line while reducing the amount of onions grown. Up until 1999, Bialas Farms still grew about 12 acres of onions. Last year they only grew about 2 acres. Orange County Onions are typically a storage onion, therefore selling them in January or February would give the farm a bit of income in the winter months. A C.S.A. is the most recent addition to the farm, with shares available in the Spring.

The family has grown a bit since it first started selling at farmers markets in 1992. The Bialas's can now boast about being a 4th Generation farm! Keep an eye open at the markets for photos of the grandkids, and even an appearance or two on a good day!

CREAMY POTATO LEEK SOUP
(courtesy of Jeff and Adina Bialas, Bialas Farms)

2 large chopped leeks, washed very well to remove all dirt
2 large peeled and thinly sliced Russet or Yukon Gold Potatoes
2 TB. butter
6-8 c. water
2 c. chicken stock or vegetable stock
salt and pepper
1 c. cream or half and half (optional)

Sauté leeks in butter over low heat for about 5 minutes, until beginning to soften. Add one teaspoon salt, continue to sauté until the leeks are soft. Cover the leeks with about 4 cups water and bring to a boil. Lower heat to a simmer, cooking for about 10 minutes. Add stock and the remainder of water, return to a simmer. Add potatoes to pot and simmer until po-

"Leeks", by Steve Blumenthal

tatoes are very soft, about 30-40 minutes. Puree with an immersion (or regular) blender. Taste for seasoning; add salt and pepper to taste. Stir in cream if desired. Serve hot. Yield 6-8 servings

---

By eating locally, they continue, you are preserving your local heritage and strengthening your community. "Farmers' markets provide a traditional local shopping venue in our global world," the Bialases write. "As we see each week, the farmers' markets are not just a place to shop, but a weekly ritual, a community gathering, a meeting place and communications hub for the entire community."

You can visit them at their farmers' markets:
Fri. in Manhattan NYC, West 97th Street between Amsterdam and Columbus Avenues
Fri. in Goshen, downtown on the green • Sat. in Pleasantville, NY, Memorial Plaza off Manville Rd. • Sat. in Ringwood, NJ, Ringwood Park and Ride Lot (Canicci Dr)

Steve Blumenthal has been drawing and painting for over 20 years and his work is in many private collections. "I love to teach" he says, "to give someone the tools and techniques to express themself." Steve is one of the founders of the Wallkill River School. He works in oils, pastels, and watercolor.

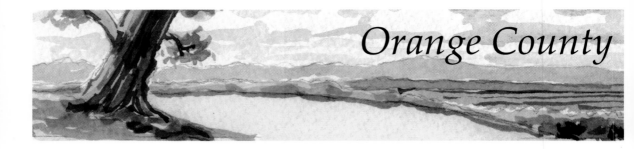

Camillo's at the Crossroads
2215 Route 208
Montgomery
457-5482

"Crossroads" by Shawn Dell Joyce.

Located at the crossroads called "Scotts Corners" of Route 208 and 17K, Camillo's is a landmark in the Town of Montgomery. Owner/Chef Chris Camillo is "old school" meaning he learned his trade well and is always in the kitchen hard at work.

Camillo's at the Crossroads features local foods on its menu, such as chickens from a Woodbridge farm, ducks from a Mountaindale farm, fish from a Forestburgh trout farm, pantry basics from Adams Fairacre Farms (the only regional farm-based grocer) and salad greens from a Newburgh wholesale farmer.

Owner Chris Camillo chooses local, because "you get a fresher product that you can actually see before you buy."

What you don't read about on Camillo's menu is that he owns his building and pays local taxes on both the restaurant and his home, also in Montgomery. He has 10 employees, mostly local youth, so his payroll stays local. He advertises in local school newspapers and donates to school functions, further spreading the local impact of money generated in his restaurant.

Camillo's is a focal point in the community and many political fundraisers, book signings, wakes, wedding parties, and other catered events happen here. The restaurant is relaxed and tranquil with a long, polished wood bar that is a popular hang for the 50-something crowd on weekend nights. The atmosphere is distinctly Montgomery, from the old maps on the wall, to the colonial-era antiques tastefully placed through the restaurant. Camillo's is one of the few Orange County restaurants that features local foods entrees right on the menu.

Bounty Cookbook

PAN ROASTED HERB AND LEMON CHICKEN (100 % natural)
(courtesy of Chris Camillo, Crossroads Restaurant)

1 whole Murray's 100% natural chicken 3-4 lbs. for 2 large servings
fresh parsley
2 sprigs of rosemary and thyme
flour for dredging
olive oil
1 oz. butter
salt and pepper
garlic (to taste) chopped
2 lemons
chicken stock

Bone chicken with sharp knife or ask your butcher. Remove the leg and thigh as one from each side of chicken. Carefully remove the drum and thigh bone from each piece leaving you with 2 boneless dark meat filets. Remove two end wing joints from both breasts, leaving the drummette on the breast. Remove both breasts from the rib cage. Now you have 2 half boneless chickens which should be marinated briefly or overnight in chopped garlic, parsley and olive oil. A quick chicken broth may be prepared by crushing the bones from the above process covering with just enough water and boil for 10 minutes. Strain and hold. All of the above can be done a day or two in advance.

Cooking your natural chicken with herbs and lemon:
Choose a sauté pan that will hold all four pieces of chicken flat. Season chicken with salt to taste .Dredge the chicken parts, skin side only, in flour. Place skin side down in your sauté pan under medium heat and start to brown and crisp the skin. Placing on the deck of your oven, just over the burner, provides for slow even cooking and crisping of the skin side. Invert when skin is golden brown and finish skin side up, if needed. Remove the chicken, prepare sauce: Drain any chicken fat from the pan roast process and add chicken broth, and juice of lemons and reduce slowly over medium to high heat to sauce consistency. Do not leave the stove during this process, it may go quickly. When sauce consistency is achieved, finish with touch of butter and fresh herbs, serve over chicken when ready. Yield 2 servings

Shawn Dell Joyce is a sustainable artist and activist, founder of the Wallkill River School, and writes a syndicated weekly column called "Sustainable Living" in the Sunday Times Herald Record. She has works in major museum collections, and private collections around the world. www.WallkillRiverSchool.com

Buck's Homestead B&B
364 Goodwill Road
Montgomery, NY 12549
(845) 457-3457
www.buckshomestead.com

"Bucks Homestead" by Leslie Waxtel

Buck's Homestead Bed & Breakfast in Montgomery fills a country farmhouse that was built around 1835, and is listed on the local register of historic places. It was the family homestead of Joan Buck Smith, who owns and runs the B&B.

While Joan was growing up, her family ran a dairy farm. She worked for years as a home and careers teacher, and found that she enjoyed cooking and entertaining - perfect vocations for a B&B entrepreneur. So, in 2006, she opened the bed and breakfast. With its welcoming porch and its warm decorations of crafts and antiques, it's a delightful home away from home.

As a farmer's daughter and a foods and nutrition teacher for 30 years, Joan knows the importance of buying local produce for her guests. She believes that the economic well-being of the community depends at least in part on supporting local farmers and businesses. And local ingredients help Joan make delicious breakfasts, including zucchini bread and apple-nut bread

"I like to use local produce for the freshness and taste," she says.

Next door to the B&B is Hoeffner's farm stand, part of which was originally Joan's father's dairy farm. In the springtimes, she says, she grows some vegetables and flowers from plants from Hoeffner's.

"My guests enjoy seeing the food grown right across the road!"

Bounty Cookbook

CORN CASSEROLE
(courtesy of Joan Buck Smith, Buck's Homestead B&B)

6 ears sweet corn
2 tablespoons butter
5 scallions, thinly sliced
2 tablespoons fresh parsley
2 eggs slightly beaten
1/2 cup half and half
1/2 teaspoon salt
1/4 teaspoon fresh-ground pepper
1 lb. medium cooked shrimp, peeled
1/4 cup flour

"Blue Corn" by Shawn Dell Joyce,
(Pastel 2006)

Preheat oven 350 degrees. Cut kernels off ears. Saute butter and green onions 2 minutes, add parsley, turn off heat. Scrape mixture in a large bowl, add corn, milk, eggs, salt and pepper. In a separate bowl, toss flour and shrimp till coated. Fold into batter. Lightly butter (or PAM) an 8 x 8" Pyrex baking dish. Pour in mixture; bake one hour till golden brown. Serve immediately. Yield 4-6 servings

*"Willie 'The Lion' Smith was born
in Goshen in 1897, and became world-famous
for the Harlem "stride" piano school.
He was a mentor to Duke Ellington, Fats Waller
and Artie Shaw among others."*

Leslie Waxtel is a painter, working in oil and watercolor. Her colorful landscapes, buildings and nature studies have been exhibited in numerous national and regional shows. She has been a demonstrating artist for the Wallkill River School and resides in Montgomery, NY.

Shawn Dell Joyce is a sustainable artist and activist, founder of the Wallkill River School, and writes a syndicated weekly column called "Sustainable Living" in the Sunday Times Herald Record. She has works in major museum collections, and private collections around the world. www.WallkillRiverSchool.com

The Old Grist Mill Restaurant
Pine Bush, NY

"The Old Grist Mill Restaurant", by Gene Bove.

Born on Halloween night in 1995, the Grist Mill Restaurant has proved to be a treat. It is the "ultimate goal of every chef to have his/her own business," says owner-chef Werner Mueller. "The journey to accomplishing that goal has been invigorating, educating, cultivating and always interesting. Leading me from Europe to Burlingham Rd. and it's been quite a trip!"

"The thing I love most about being a chef is taking inexpensive ingredients and integrating different combinations of herbs, spices, and foods to create something that is out of this world!" Mueller likens cooking to painting a masterpiece or composing a symphony. "In a chef's world—that is the ultimate triumph."

Mueller is grateful for access to the freshest ingredients in the Hudson Valley through farm markets. "For the farmer, chef, and consumer; it is a win-win situation when people eat locally." Mueller also points out that eating locally has to extend beyond the farm and the home. "Fast food restaurants are slowly putting Mom & Pop restaurants on the endangered species list."

Restaurants like the Old Grist Mill ensure variety of flavors, creativity in food, and cultural diversity. If people "continue to choose the franchises over Mom & Pop restaurants, we will be destined to dine in a boring, mundane, Orwellian world where everything tastes and looks the same."

Mueller wants his restaurant to be an island in the fast paced world where "we want everything done yesterday." He hopes diners will savor this culinary journey, not rush through it. "Life is too short not to be able to slow down, pause and enjoy our food!"

Bounty Cookbook

PAN ROASTED CHICKEN BREAST FILLED WITH GOAT CHEESE, SUN-DRIED TOMATOES AND SPINACH
(courtesy of Werner Mueller, Chef-Proprietor The Old Grist Mill Restaurant)

4 Large Local Chicken Breasts
10 oz. Local Goat Cheese
10 oz. Fresh Spinach (blanched)
6 oz. Sun-dried Tomatoes (soaked)
10 oz. Fresh Basil Leaves
1/4 C. Olive Oil
1 C. Sweet Butter
1 tsp. Garlic (thinly sliced)
1 C. Chicken Stock
Salt & Pepper

Carefully cut pockets in chicken breasts. In a bowl, fold goat cheese, spinach, sun-dried tomatoes, basil,

Salt, and pepper together. Stuff chicken breasts with filling. Sear breasts in hot olive oil, first skin down then turn, bake in an oven at 375 degrees for about 15 mins. Take out of pan, and drain. Add half of the butter and garlic to the pan. Stir until garlic browns, and add chicken stock. Reduce stock to half amount. Whisk in the rest of the cold butter. Slice the chicken breast and serve with roasted garlic pan juices. Guten Appetite!

"Port Jervis was the first stop on the "Old Mine Road"
known as the first 100 mile road in America.
The road was built by Dutch settlers who sought mines of gold
and copper along the Delaware River Highlands."

Gene Bove-A former advertising art director, Gene has been painting with The Wallkill River School for seven years. He feels blessed to live in the foothills of the beautiful Shawangunk Mountain range which inspire him to paint all the fields, farms and mountains which he holds so dear.

GREENS AND BEANS
(courtesy of Ann Knapp)

1 lb. escarole, chicory, kale or Swiss chard (the
only one needed to be stripped is kale)
1/4 cup olive oil
1 medium chopped onion
3 chopped garlic cloves
1 lb. 13 oz. can of Goya kidney or white beans or
what you like
4 strips of bacon, chopped (optional)
salt and pepper to taste
parsley, basil or other herbs

Cut greens in one inch pieces. Add to 2 quarts of boiling water, cook about 10 min. Drain water – reserve about 1 cup of liquid – you may need to add it – depending on how you like it. In pan add oil, bacon, onion, garlic. Sauté about 5 minutes. Add the greens and stir gently - about 5 minutes.

Lastly – add beans, juice and all – stir with greens. Taste again and add more herbs if needed. Sprinkle with parmesan cheese and serve with crusty bread.
Yield 2 servings

"Frederick Franck, a world-class artist and author created a sanctuary and sculpture park he called Pacem in Terris (Peace on Earth), home to sculptures of the Buddha, Christ, and other representations of what he identified as the "True Human," which still exists today, at his home in Warwick."

Bounty Cookbook

PUMPKIN CHOCOLATE CHIP BREAD
(courtesy of Alice Nash Oc tourism)

2 cup sugar
4 eggs
1-1/4 cup oil
2 cup cooked pumpkin
3 cup sifted flour
1/2 teaspoon salt
1/2 teaspoon cinnamon
2 teaspoon baking soda
2 teaspoon baking powder
1 cup mini chocolate chips

"Ronnie's Still Life" by Ronnie Mehrberg Lipitz.

Mix by hand in large bowl: sugar, eggs, baking soda, baking powder, cinnamon, salt. Add pumpkin – mix in. Add oil and stir until all oil is blended in. Put in flour 1 cup at a time, blending in after each cup. Add chips last and blend them in. Grease 2 loaf pans and fill half. Bake at 375 degrees until toothpick comes out clean (about 50 min.). Make 2 loaves

UPSIDE-DOWN PEAR ALMOND COBBLER
(courtesy of Denise Heude)

1/3 cup almond paste
1/3 cup sugar
1/4 cup softened butter
2 eggs
1 teaspoon vanilla
1/4 cup flour
8 peeled, cored, ripe pear halves.

Beat first three ingredients with mixer at high speed until creamy. Lower speed, beat 2 eggs and 1 tsp. vanilla. Stir in flour. Spread in a greased 1 quart quiche dish. Top with pear halves. Bake at 350 for 40 minutes. Yield 6-8 servings

Ronnie Mehrberg Lipitz-A Former High School art teacher. Studied art at Adelphi University, Pratt, Parsons, FIT, and SVA. Is currently painting at the Art Student's league and with The Wallkill River School of Painting. She lives in New York City and In Sugarloaf, N.Y.

SQUASH AND RED BEAN SOUP
(courtesy of Marie Claude Gracia's cook book, LeMoulin Poudenas France)

1 lb. red and black beans
1/2 lb. ham on a bone
2 slices thick bacon with more fat
1 or 2 slices smoked ham
1 ham bone or ham hock (optional)
1/2 lb. squash
4 potatoes
4 carrots
1 small stick celery
5 sprigs parsley
1 large onion
2 cloves
1 bay leaf
1 sprig thyme
salt and pepper

"Ferme Rouge", by Jean Claude Gracia

Place all the beans in a big pot of cold water and let stand for 12 hours; change the water several times; the beans must be very swelled. Place all the meat except the smoked ham in a pot of cold water and bring to a boil for 5 minutes until the meat is white then remove and drain all the pieces. Clean the pot and drop again the meat in 6 quarts of cold water. Add all the beans, vegetables peeled but not cut; squash peeled and diced, potatoes, carrots, and stick of celery. Then add parsley, the onion peeled where you already inserted the cloves, bay leaf, thyme, salt and pepper; bring just to a boil; reduce heat and simmer 1-1/2 hours the cover half way. Then add the slice of thick bacon and simmer for 1-1/2 hours. When it's ready, remove the meat on a plate, the aromatic herbs on another plate; and the soup in a tureen.
Yields 8 servings.

Jean Claude Gracia, passionate about people, farmers and the land, was born in 1958 in a small village of Gascony in France. He studied at the art school in Biarritz, and then traveled around the world. Now, he has homes in the U.S. and in France. Paintings by Gracia hang in private and corporate collections and in museums and galleries around the world.

Bounty Cookbook

STUFFED SWISS CHARD
(courtesy of Kate Fox, Watershed Learning Center at Kezialain Farm, Westtown)

1/2 C. Minced Celery
1/3 C. Chopped Walnuts
6 C. Cooked rice (Brown
        basmati is best)
2 Tbsp. Fresh Parsley (chopped)
1 Large onion (chopped)
1 1/2 C. Cottage cheese
1/2 C. Local Feta cheese
        (crumbled)
2 Local eggs
12 Large Swiss chard leaves
Salt, pepper, Italian
        seasonings to taste

Combine rice with chopped walnuts, celery, onion, cheeses, eggs and spices. Wash Chard leaves.

Renee Bonagura is a student at Goshen Middle School. Her artistic skills in painting and drawing awarded her a spot in the 8th grade Advanced Art class. Renee hopes to use her artistic abilities to become an Architect.

Trim away center stalks so that leaves can be rolled. Place 3-5 Tbsp. of filling on each leaf, and roll or wrap. Place seam side down in oiled pan, secure with toothpicks if necessary. Pour water in pan until it is 1/2 in. deep. Cover tightly. Cook 45 mins. At 375 degrees. Yield 2 servings

"A popular outing around 1910 was a trip to Cuddebackville to watch D.W. Griffith filming one of his silent movies there. Griffith has been hailed as the father of modern day cinema, a great innovator and artist who invented many of the cinematic techniques still used today. Movie greats like Max Sennet and Mary Pickford made the trip to Orange County."

GARLIC AND KALE SOUP
(courtesy of Marge Corrieri, Blooming
Hill Farm)

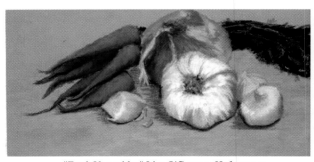

"Fresh Vegetables" Lisa O'Gorman-Hofsommer

8 c. vegetable stock
4 TB. minced garlic
2 -3 TB. extra virgin olive oil
1 TB. paprika
2 sprigs fresh sage
2-3 sprigs fresh thyme
1 bunch kale
1/2 c. dried orzo
small bunch of fresh parsley tied in a bundle (about 10 sprigs)
salt and freshly ground pepper to taste
freshly grated Parmigianino-Romano cheese

In a large soup pot, sauté the garlic in the olive oil till golden. Add the stock, stir in
the paprika, sage, thyme and parsley bundle. Bring the broth to a boil and simmer
for 15 minutes. While the broth is simmering, wash, and remove the large stem and
vein from each piece of kale. Cut the kale into small pieces so that it will be easy to
eat with a spoon. In a separate pot, cook the orzo according to package directions.
Drain and set aside. Remove the parsley, sage and thyme from the garlic broth. Add
the kale to the broth and cook for about 3 minutes. Add the cooked orzo to the soup
pot. Season to taste with salt and pepper. Pass the grated cheese to top the soup. This
soup is delicious the first day, and even better when reheated on the second day.

"Lucille Ball made her stage debut at the Ritz Theatre
in Newburgh in 1941. Ella Fitgerald, Milton Berle,
and Frank Sinatra also performed there."

Lisa O'Gorman-Hofsommer was born & raised in Yonkers, N.Y. She moved to the Hudson Valley in 1990. She has been painting in
pastels since then, and has strong desire to paint wildlife & landscapes. She has a Pet Portraits business. <Petportraitsnmore.com>

Bounty Cookbook

GRANDPA'S POTATO SALAD
(courtesy of Ellen Trayer)

5 lbs. potatoes
1 lb. sour cream
2 c. mayonnaise
1/4 lb. bacon -- fried crisp
2 TB. bacon fat
1 TB. vinegar
4 oz. pimento chopped
1 medium onion chopped
salt and pepper

"Heirloom Potatoes" Shawn Dell Joyce is a sustainable artist and activist, founder of the Wallkill River School.

Boil potatoes till done. Meanwhile mix together sour cream, mayonnaise, (start with 1-1/2 pints of each and add more if needed) salt & pepper, chopped onion, chopped pimentos. Crumble bacon into mayonnaise mixture. Add bacon fat and vinegar. When you can handle the potatoes peel them and either slice or chunk them, warm, into mayonnaise. Refrigerate. Yields 12 servings.

SWEET POTATO SALAD
(courtesy of Marge Corrieri, Blooming Hill Farm)

1 1/2 lbs. sweet potatoes
1 TB. mayonnaise
1 TB. poupon mustard
salt to taste • 1/4 tsp. freshly ground black pepper
2 large celery stalks, finely chopped
1/2 c. chopped dill pickle
1/2 c. chopped canned pineapple (use fresh if available)
1/4 c. finely chopped pecans, toasted
1/2 c. finely chopped red onion
chives cut up – for garnish

Bake the sweet potatoes at 400 degrees for about 50 minutes. Test with a fork to see if tender. Cool and peel. Cut into about 1/2 inch chunks. In a large bowl, mix the mayonnaise, mustard, salt and pepper to blend. Add the sweet potato cubes, celery, pickle, pineapple, pecans and onion to the mayonnaise in the large bowl. Toss gently until coated. Sprinkle with the chives and serve. Yields 5 cups.

Orange County

ORANGE COUNTY TAMALES
(courtesy of Shawn Dell Joyce)

Dried corn husks (available in Mexican grocers or imported foods aisle on
 the supermarket)
2 c. Masa de Harina (corn flour)
1/3 c. pesto or 1/3 c. olive oil
1 c. fresh basil
clove garlic
1 zucchini (optional) grated
1/2 c. corn kernels (frozen from the summer's harvest is best)
1 c. sun-dried or dehydrated tomatoes (from the summer harvest)
8 oz. ball of fresh mozzarella Cheese cut into long rectangles

Soak corn husks in a large pot filled with water for 20 minutes. While they are soaking, combine oil, garlic and basil in a food processor or blender, add in zucchini if
you have it, then add Masa a bit at a time until it forms a stiff dough. Empty dough
into a bowl. Lay out cheese slices and dried tomatoes on a cutting board. Arrange
everything so that it is within reach. Start with a wet corn husk and put about 1/3
cup of dough in the center. Flatten the dough with your fingers, lay two dried
tomato strips end-to-end, and a strip of mozzarella on top. Fold the corn husk over so
that you are making a "taco" with the cheese and tomato inside. Wrap the edges of the
corn husk together and tuck the loose end underneath to form a small packet. Place
packet in a steamer. Repeat this process until you have used up all the corn husks
and dough. Use the same pot the corn husks were soaking in to steam the tamales.
Boil the water then place the steamer in the pot and allow to steam for 20 minutes.
Cheese may ooze from the corn husks. Remove tamales from steamer, and allow to
cool enough to handle. Eat tamales by removing the corn husk. Tamales can be re-
frigerated and microwaved later. Tamales make a good "brown bag lunch" since they
don't need any other wrapper or container other than the corn husk. A very "green"
meal! Yields 8-10 servings.

*"Port Jervis got its name as a stop on
the Delaware and Hudson Canal, and for John B. Jervis
the chief engineer on the canal."*

Orange County Bounty Cookbook

Winter

(January, February, March)

What's in season?

Fruits

        Apples (cold storage)

        Apple Cider

Vegetables

        Cabbage (Cold storage)

        Carrots (Cold storage)

        Herbs (dried)

        Lettuces (greenhouse)

        Onions (cold storage)

        Potatoes (cold storage)

        Winter Squash (cold storage)

        Turnips (cold storage)

Meats

        Chicken, Turkey, Pheasant

        Pork, Beef, Venison

        Honey

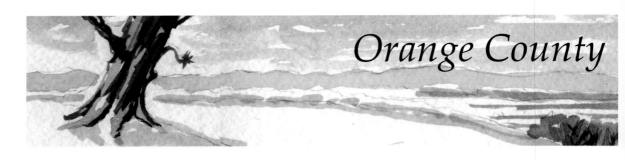

"Eating Local in the Winter"
by Shawn Dell Joyce

In the dead of winter, most of us dream of the plump ripe tomatoes of summer, while fondling the pink excuses for tomatoes in the supermarkets. But, did you realize how many local farms are open right now with some fresh, locally-grown produce? Here's a partial listing of a few farms in the region where you can stop in all winter and what they offer.

Brother and sister team; Holly and Ned Roebuck, are working together to save their family farm. For several generations Roebucks have worked this particular piece of property into many different configurations. These Roebucks have free ranging Belted Galloway cows, and an organic vegetable farm. *Walnut Grove Farm* in the Town of Crawford, offers frozen organic free-range beef, pork, bacon, pies and jars of jams and jellies by appointment. Ned Roebuck (845) 313-4855 **www.WalnutGroveFarms.net**

A family farm for many generations, *W. Rogowski Farm*, 327-329 Glenwood Road, Pine Island, 258-4423, has an organic farm stand open year round. The owner/farmer is Cheryl Rogowski and family, and has been a major force in promoting sustainable agriculture in our region. You can currently find apples, pears, shallots, turnips, beets, garlic, onions (of course) potatoes, greens of many varieties including Asian, chili peppers, squashes, turnips, radishes, cabbages, dried beans, and processed things like jellies, honey, maple syrup, sugar and crème. Also you will find books, my artwork, and some garlic wreaths. Will be open after Jan. 13 every Sat. from 9-2 until spring. **www.rogowskifarm.com**

Nestled between subdivisions, and making the most of a bit of open space is *Blooming Hill Farm,* 1251 Route 208, in Washingtonville. Guy Jones and sister, Cindy Jones offer many varieties of potatoes, squash, cold-hardy lettuce, and chards, root vegetables, onions, broccoli some fruits, eggs, and real milk with real cream on top. You must see the farm stand to believe the beauty and abundance of these fresh organic vegetables. Open Sat. from 9-2 through April. 782-7310 **www.bloominghillfarm.com**

Dolan's Farm in Gardiner is on 208 near Ireland Corners. I would give you their phone number but it won't do you much good, because no one answers the phone on this busy farm. You are more likely to find the farmer around back behind the farm stand in the

Bounty Cookbook

packing room where bins of apples are available. Dolan's is open, and you can buy apples until this season's harvest runs out. Just pull down the driveway a bit and look for a lanky smiling man up to his elbows in tractor parts and you've found Mr. Dolan.

Apples are also crisp and delicious from *Soons Orchards*, 23 Soons Circle, New Hampton. Soons is probably famous for their pies, but you can find local garlic, vegetables, apples, pears, fresh ground peanut or almond butter, mixes for dips or soups, jars of salsa, jam and jellies, honey, and maple syrup, among other items. Soons is open to the public until 5 pm most days, and encourages you order pies in advance for the holidays. Soons has been family owned and operated for many years, and you can almost always find a Soons in the store. **www.SoonsOrchards.com**, (845) 374-5471

One of the few multigenerational working family farms left in the region is Cornwall's *Jones Farm* on 190 Angola Road. This farm does a bustling business in the winter with the "largest gift store in the region," according to co-owner David Clearwater. He and wife Terry, and her parents are the farmers. Terry is also an artist and framer who runs a frame shop next to the farm store. Their farm features fresh fall apples, homemade fudge, a bakery, gourmet foods, and many other goodies. Open 8am-5pm weekends, and until 6pm during the week. **www.JonesFarmInc.com,** (845) 534-4445

Dines Farm offers fresh meats, and other farm's products delivered to your door! Dines is located in Oak Hill, about 38 miles South of Albany, and offers their own pasture-raised chicken, pork, lamb, beef, duck, rabbit, turkey, chicken sausage, and hot dogs. Right now, they are offering mushrooms, goat cheese, and jams and jellies from other farms. Dines delivery network is mostly Rockland, Westchester, Orange, and parts of Ulster. They are open to delivering in other areas, so it is worth a call if you want them to come to you. To set up a deliver, or ask what's available, call (518) 239-4206 or email **dinesfarm@aol.com** and ask to be on the emailing list.

This is not a complete list, because I certainly don't know all the farmers or even all that may keep winter hours. If I missed one, please let me know.

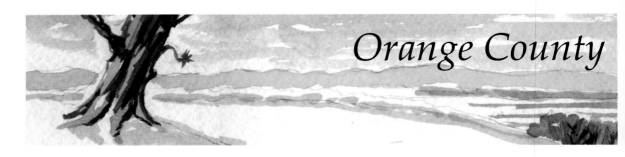

"Tips for a Greener Kitchen"
by Shawn Dell Joyce

How you prepare all those fresh local foods has as much impact on your health (and the environment) as your food choices. Greening your kitchen involves conscious consumption; being aware of the energy and resources you are consuming while preparing your meals. Something as simple as replacing clunky old appliances with energy star rated appliances will save you $100 or more on your yearly electric bill. Using these appliances consciously will reduce your energy usage.

- Propane is more efficient than electric ranges and ovens.
- Don't use the oven in the middle of a hot day, especially if you have an air conditioner on.
- Turn the burner off 2 minutes before the pasta is done, and let it cook the rest of the way using residual heat.
- If you have to heat the oven, have a batch of cookies ready to go in when the roast comes out. Turn off the oven, and let the residual heat bake the cookies.
- There is no need to preheat an oven unless you are baking scones that depend on a hot oven. Otherwise, add a few minutes to the cooking time and eliminate the preheating time.
- Don't place a heat producing appliance like an oven or dishwasher touching a refrigerator.
- Plug microwaves and other appliances with digital read outs or square plugs into a power strip. These appliances create phantom loads that suck energy from your outlets even when they are turned off.

Imagine if you had to carry your day's supply of water on your head. Most of us use more than 55 gallons just to cook, drink, bathe and flush every day. Many people around the world start their day by walking miles to find freshwater then carrying it home in a vessel on their head. How conscientiously would you use water if that was your life?

- keep a bowl in the sink and only use enough water to fill the bowl. Instead of dumping the dirty water down the drain, carry the bowl to the window and water the shrubs.
- Use water more than once. If you are boiling potatoes, put corn in a steamer on top of the pot. You can boil green beans in the same water.

Bounty Cookbook

- If there is a small amount of water leftover in your glass, pour it into a pet's bowl, or a plant instead of down the drain.
- Run the dishwasher only if it's fully loaded, and don't rinse the dishes first unless they are caked with food.
- Buy low flow plumbing fixtures, and faucet aerators that conserve water.

We throw out enough plastic wrap every year to shrink wrap the state of Texas. A truly green kitchen has no plastic or paper products. Conserve limited resources and energy by eliminating one time use items like paper towels, napkins or plastic bags. Spend a little money and effort on the real deal.

- Have cloth napkins and washable hand towels instead of paper.
- Use ceramic or glass bowls instead of plastic bags and containers.
- Don't buy bottled water instead buy a good glass container with a lid and a filter for your tap water if necessary.
- Try parchment paper instead of plastic wrap and aluminum foil.
- Use waxed paper bags instead of plastic bags for packing lunches or leftovers.
- Precycle; before you purchase an item, buy the product with the least packaging.
- Recycle; set up bins in a convenient place for the whole family.
- Keep a set of tote bags on a hook by the door or in your car for grocery shopping.

The single biggest thing you can do to green your kitchen is to compost. A full third of bagged household waste is organic matter that could have been composted. Use a ceramic crock on your counter, or a large bowl with a tight-fitting lid. All vegetable scraps, eggshells, coffee grounds, peels and organic matter (that did not originate from an animal) go into the crock. At the end of the day, the crock gets emptied into the compost bin or pile in the backyard. A couple of chickens will help the process along, and give you some eggs in return.

If you spend good money on high quality produce and organic ingredients, you don't want to wash it in a sink laden with phosphate-based detergents. Instead, buy natural detergents that won't harm your landscaping when you pour out used dishwater. Avoid any soap containing antibacterial detergents, or toilet bowl cleaners containing bleach if you have a septic system. Instead, use vinegar and baking soda as an abrasive cleaner for sinks and toilets. A green kitchen is a conscious kitchen. Live consciously and gently on the earth!

Chateau Hathorn

33 Hathorn Road
Warwick, New York 10990
(845) 986-6099
www.chateauhathorn.com

"Chateau Hathorn" by Chrissy Pahucki

Trained as a chef in Switzerland, Dolph Zuenger always admired the United States. The feeling was so strong and so protracted that in time, he and his wife, Helene, decided to move here. Dolph would pursue his career as a chef in America.

The Zuengers opened their first restaurant 31 years ago. Seven years later, they bought the Chateau Hathorn.

The thing that Dolph most loves about being a chef, he says, "is making people happy. I enjoy being creative with my recipes and in most cases, my customers have been coming to us for years."

It's like meeting old friends, he says. There's little that's better in life than having people come together to celebrate, to enjoy life and each other. The best of times, Dolph believes, are the weddings. Being part of the promise, part of the start of a new life, there's nothing like it. And then, he says, he gets to see them on the anniversaries, too.

Local produce and local foods are part of the picture at the Chateau. "I think people should take advantage of what they have in their own backyards," Dolph says, "and eating locally is part of that."

Dolpe would like people to know that the chateau is open for dinner Wednesday through Saturday from 5 p.m. until 10 p.m. and on Sunday from 3 p.m. until 8 p.m. In addition to a wonderful menu selection, he says, the restaurant has specials that change daily.

Bounty Cookbook

POACHED COD "HATHORN"
(courtesy of Dolph Zueger)

Cod is a very light, not-fishy fish, which makes it similar to our lake fish in Switzerland. Also, in Switzerland, it is very popular to poach fish.

4 filets of cod, each piece approximately 8-10 oz.
2 c. dry white wine
1 lemon
1/2 onion chopped
3 cloves garlic chopped
2 tomatoes chopped
2 TB. chopped basil or parsley
freshly ground pepper and salt

For the sauce:
2 tsp. cornstarch • 2 oz. heavy cream • 1 cup chicken stock

Preheat oven to 400 degrees. Spray a baking dish with "Pam" or similar product.

Place filets in pan and pour white wine over the top. Sprinkle evenly with chopped onion, garlic, tomatoes, basil or parsley. Season with salt and pepper to your liking.

Bake in oven, uncovered, for 6 to 10 mins., depending on thickness of filets.

Remove fish from pan after cooking and place remaining liquid in a saucepan. Stir in chicken stock and heavy cream. When blended, whisk in cornstarch.

Garnish fish with more chopped parsley or basil before serving. Best served with salted potatoes or noodles.

The recipe can be adjusted to your taste buds should you prefer another seasoning, or a vegetable stock as opposed to chicken stock. Yield 6 servings

Chrissy Pahucki was born in Goshen, New York in 1975. She received a Bachelors degree in Art Education from Buffalo State College and a Masters Degree from the State University in New Paltz. Chrissy Pahucki is both an artist and art educator who teaches art to students at the C. J. Hooker Goshen Middle School. She spends her most of the summer outdoors, playing with her three young children, camping and taking photographs to inspire her paintings.

Kiernan Farm

1308 Bruynswick Road
Gardiner, NY
(845) 255-5995
www.kiernanfarm.com

"Kiernan Farm", by Gene Bove.

Back in 1982, Marty Kiernan bought a 140-acre farm, planning to raise horses. He and his wife Thelma ended up raising Shane, Ryan and Keri there; raising beef; and opening a B&B.

Kiernan Farm has been raising beef since 2001. For Marty, the appeal is the freedom. He's outside, he's in the open, and he's making decisions, responsible for success.

Thelma operates Blueberry Inn on Kiernan Farm, a successful B&B, run in the circla-1800 farmhouse. For her, the attraction is in meeting people from all over the world, cooking for them, learning from them and teaching them. Thelma lets them know about the farm, its history and its grass-fed, grass-finished beef.

It's a great site for a B&B, Thelma says, a lovely old house with a view of the mountain from the back lawn. "Add in agriculture - our guests enjoy watching the cows graze - and you get agri-tourism," she says.

For Marty, local eating translates into preserving open space. If you want it in your community, you either have to use tax money to buy the development rights, or the consumers have to make the decision to buy the products that grow on that open space. Otherwise, that space will just be gone. Simple as that.

Thelma adds another thought. Locally grown food is simply better. "It's better for the consumer, it's better-tasting, and it's better for the cattle." Thelma adds that the beef, which is inspected by the USDA, can be bought right at the farm. Customers call in their orders - large or small - and the Kiernans set an appointment for when they can pick it up.

The Kiernans treasure what they produce. It's "completely grass-raised beef," Marty says. "Not one molecule of any type of grain is fed to our cows. No steroids. No antibiotics."

CROCK POT ROAST
(courtesy of Thelma Kiernan--Kiernan Farm and Blueberry Inn,)

1 Chuck Roast (about 2 lbs.)
1 tsp. extra virgin olive oil
1 1/2 c. vegetable juice
1 1/2 tsp. Worcestershire sauce
pinch of salt
pinch of pepper
2-3 bay leaves, whole
1 large onion, sliced _ inch thick
1 8 oz. – 10 oz. box of mushrooms, sliced 1/4 inch thick
3/4 c. water
2 TBS. flour

Heat extra virgin olive oil in a hot pan. Season roast with salt and pepper on both sides. Sear chuck roast in oil on both sides.

Place roast in crock pot and layer the next 7 ingredients in order listed. Heat in crock-pot 2 1/2 hours on high and 6-7 hours on low or until meat is fork tender.

Mix water and flour, add to crock-pot and stir. Heat for a 1/2 hour more. Serve over egg noodles or fresh mashed potatoes. Yield 4-6 servings

The Shawangunk Ridge is one of the
most popular climbing areas in North America,
visited by 50,000 climbers per year.

Gene Bove-A former advertising art director, Gene has been painting with The Wallkill River School for seven years. He feels blessed to live in the foothills of the beautiful Shawangunk Mountain range which inspire him to paint all the fields, farms and mountains which he holds so dear.

Captain's Table of Monroe
547 Route 17M
Monroe, NY 10950
(845) 783-0209
www.captains-table.com

For Ray Hafenecker, the owner of the Captain's Table, a summer job turned into a life's journey. In 2007, the landmark restaurant celebrates 35 years of service in Monroe.

The restaurant, which these days is about an hour's drive from New York

"Captains Table" by Bruce Thorne

City, began as a roadside rest stop for travelers along old Route 17. Hafenecker says that listening to the clientele has brought the restaurant its growth and success. For instance, a few years ago, Hafenecker installed a 1/3 of an acre sand beach adjacent to the restaurant. The plan had been to use it for volleyball, but dinner guests took it over as a play spot. The kids can spend their time on the "beach," while parents sit nearby, enjoying themselves as adults.

"A beer- $4. Dinner - $14.95. Memories - Priceless," Hafenecker says.

Of all that he loves about the restaurant, Hafenecker says that, for him, the best part is responding to challenges and changes, finding ways to adapt and to refine the business.

And while chain restaurants proliferate in the Mid-Hudson Valley, challenging the independent operator, people are waking up to the idea of eating local foods and supporting restaurants that use local foods, and the farms that supply them. "Population growth should fuel an increase in demand for products and services in Orange County," he says. "Quality products and local means 'fresh,'" he says.

Bounty Cookbook

FRENCH ONION SOUP
(courtesy of Ray Hafenecker, Captain's Table)

Onions
Garlic
Brandy
Salt
Pepper
Beef Soup base

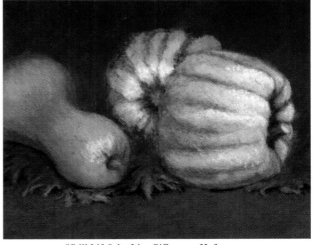

"Still Life", by Lisa O'Gorman-Hofsommer

Bring to boil in large chef's pot, Onions, Garlic, Brandy, Salt, Pepper and Beef Soup Base. Cook for 30 minutes. Serve im crock covering croutons with mozzarella and swiss cheese.
Yield 2 or more servings

"According to Rutgers-Newark Geology Professor Alexander Gates; rock outcroppings found in Harriman State Park appear to be a good geological match for the type of rock in Brazil. This is evidence of continental drift from over 600 million years ago."

Bruce Thorne-His style has been compared to Van Gogh for his rich color, thick impasto paint technique and his passion for painting.

Lisa O'Gorman-Hofsommer was born & raised in Yonkers, N.Y. She moved to the Hudson Valley in 1990. She has been painting in pastels since then, and has strong desire to paint wildlife & landscapes. She has a Pet Portraits business. <Petportraitsnmore.com>

Crystal Inn
12 Amity Road
Warwick, NY 10990
(845) 258-9083
www.crystalinn.dine.com

The Crystal Inn was established in 1965 by present owner Casmier "Gus" Zygmunt. It has stayed in the family, and is now run by general manager Ryan Zygmunt.

"Crystal Inn", watercolor by James Amore.

As Warwick has grown and changed over the years, so too has the Inn. At first, it was a local roadside tavern. Over time, it has become a regional dining destination, earning a four-star rating and being named by the Times Herald-Record as one of the top 10 restaurants in the Mid-Hudson Valley.

Chef James M. Haurey enjoys the creativity that comes with using fresh organic and local produce, often hand-picked by him moments before he cooks it. He whips the produce into the fresh, bright and eclectic contemporary American-style dishes on his menu.

The Crystal Inn believes that it's important for local people and restaurants to use produce from local farms, not only to benefit the local economy, but also to promote - to local customers and travelers - the quality of locally grown, extremely fresh, and wonderfully healthy fruits and vegetables.

The Crystal Inn describes itself as a unique dining destination. Its comfortable and relaxed atmosphere allows diners to have quick casual meals from the pub menu, not only enjoy "but also to delight in extremely creative and award-winning cuisine which has gained the chef very high marks and national acclaim, all without having to get 'decked out'."

Bounty Cookbook

CREAMY PINE ISLAND ONION SOUP
(courtesy of Crystal Inn)

4 medium Pine Island onions, sliced thin
1/2lb. salted, sweet cream butter
4 tbsp extra virgin olive oil
1 bottle dry white wine
1/2qt heavy cream
Salt
Black pepper
1 small bunch of chives, sliced paper thin
2 flowering chives, flowers picked

In a stainless steel pot, on low heat add the butter & olive oil, toss in the onions & season lightly with salt & pepper. Let cook as slow as possible to intensify the natural sugars in the onion, try not to color the onions. A little color is ok, the more you color the onions the deeper & richer the soup will be. In this case, it should be lighter and fresher, so avoid coloring the onions. When the onions have cooked completely down add _ of the bottle of wine & turn the heat up to a simmer, and allow white wine to reduce by about 50%. Add the heavy cream & let reduce to about 1/3 original amt. When the cream has cooked down, taste, & adjust the salt & pepper to taste as needed. Add contents to a blender & puree until velvety smooth. Return to a clean pot until all the soup has been pureed & bring back up to serving temperature. When ready to serve split the soup up into 6 bowls & garnish with the sliced chives, chive flowers, garlic croutons & a fresh crack of black pepper. Enjoy! Yield 6 servings

*"The rich dark soil of the Black Dirt region was created
by the three mile thick glaciers depositing nutrients
as it melted after the Ice Age."*

James M. Amore is an Orange County Resident who graduated from SUNY New Paltz with a degree in art education. Over the past 3 decades, experience with paintings and drawings have garnered ribbons in several juried shows including best in shows, work in private collections and used in numerous publications.

Hill Hold Museum
Campbell Hall, NY

"Hill Hold Montage" by Steve Blumenthal

Hill Hold Museum is the historic homestead built by prosperous farmer, Thomas Bull, in 1769. A tour of the 18th century stone house and various 19th century outbuildings, including the 1870 one room school house, allows visitors to step back in time to see what country life was like for the early settlers to Orange County. Visitors have an opportunity to learn how rural families needs for food, clothing and fuel all came from the farm.

The Georgian style home, which was occupied by members of the Bull-Jackson family for over 200 years before it was donated to the Orange County Parks Department in 1969, was painstakingly restored back to it's 18th century form in the 1970's. The gracious farmhouse retains all of the original woodwork and paneling, wide plank floors, fireplaces and many period furnishings that belonged to the family.

Hill Hold affords visitors a taste of Hudson Valley farm life in the late 18th and early 19th centuries with various period buildings, artifacts, antique tools and decorative arts plus the resident farm animals all in bucolic setting with rolling pastures and mature trees.

"Sally's Dream Playground in Thomas Bull Memorial Park
next to the Orange County Gold Course is named after
Sally McGlynn, an activist for handicapped rights.
The playground is accessible for all abilities
with ramps, and special equipment.."

Bounty Cookbook

CHOCOLATE CAKE
(courtesy of Amy Bull Crist (My grandmother's favorite dessert))

CHOCOLATE PORTION
2 squares Bakers Chocolate
1 egg yolk
1/2 cup sweet milk

Cook until it thickens and then add to
cake portion

CAKE PORTION
1-1/2 cup sugar
1/2 cup butter
2 eggs
1/2 cup milk
1 teaspoon baking soda
2 cup flour

"Hill Hold Museum" by William Noonan.

Mix two portions and bake in two layers at 375 degrees for about 20 min.

CHOCOLATE ICING
2 squares Baker's Chocolate
1-1/2 cup sugar
1/2 cup milk
1 pinch cream of tartar

Cook until mixture forms a soft ball in water. Add 1 teaspoon of vanilla
   Yield 6-8 servings

Steve Blumenthal has been drawing and painting for over 20 years and his work is in many private collections. " I love to teach" he says,
"to give someone the tools and techniques to express themself" Steve is one of the founders of the Wallkill River School. He works in oils,
pastels, and watercolor.

William Noonan is a artist who resides and works in Orange County. He is known for his loose brushwork and sophisticated use of color.
You can see examples of his work on his website at www.williamnoonan.com.

Downtown Breads
& Bake Shop

63 Clinton Street
Montgomery, NY

"Downtown Breads" by Marge Morales.

As the artisanal food trend blossomed in the garden of our overstressed world, Downtown Breads & Bake Shop came into being. It was March 2007, and who had time to bake? For those who love the sweets and starches, it's all too easy to skip the homemade and go for the commerical. Downtown Breads saw the need for all-natural, preservative-free, additive-free baked goods, right there in Montgomery.

At the bakery, the chefs and bakers love selling high-quality, all-natural products. The attraction of healthy, local baked goods draws customers, and keeps the local economy thriving.

The bakery folks want people to know that, "We are customer-friendly and will accomodate your need for home-baked goods."

"The Verplanck Room at the
Metropolitan Museum of Art was constructed
from the 18th century
Colden Mansion in Montgomery."

Bounty Cookbook

FLOURLESS PEANUT BUTTER COOKIES (no gluten)
(courtesy of Downtown Breads and Bake Shop)

1 lb. peanut butter
1 c. sugar
pinch of salt
3 local farm egg whites-stiffened

Whip peanut butter, sugar and salt till fluffy. Fold into egg whites. Roll mixture into balls the size of a gumball. (Balls may be rolled in sugar or you may press fork in sugar first.) Place on a lined cookie sheet about 2 inches apart and press down with fork. Bake at 325 for 10-12 minutes. Yield 3 dozen servings

"Maybrook was once known as the "transportation hub of the Northeast" because the largest rail hub was built there in 1910. It was open until 1974 employing 1,500 people at its peak. Yellow Freight now occupies the area where the hub once was."

"Orange County Bounty", Pastel by Mary Sealfon.

Marge Morales of Rock Tavern sees herself as a modern-day storyteller, using paint as her medium. In oils and watercolors, Marge offers more than images; her art tells stories that touch the heart and the soul.

Mary Mugele Sealfon received a BA in painting at the U of California at Santa Barbara and a MA from NYU. In New York City she pursued a career as an Art Director and designer. She has won numerous awards and her paintings and prints have been exhibited nationally and internationally. She also teaches art locally, including SUNY Orange.

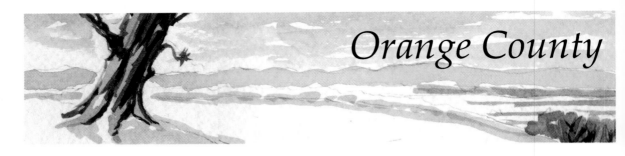

Lupinksi Farm
1 Houston Rd
Goshen, NY
(845) 361-1429

In the early 1930s, Diana Lupinski's husband's grandfather, Joseph Lupinski, was working the family farm in Goshen as a tenant farmer with his sons John W. and Barney. In time, John W., took over the task.

In 1957, John W. bought the farm and continued to run it as a dairy farm until his wife Theresa passed away.

"Lupinski Farm" by Marge Morales.

There has always been little money in dairy farming and, Lupinski says, "Dairy is a 365-day 24/7 job with no breaks or vacations. Vegetables in the northeast are more seasonal."

And so, Lupinski Farms made the transition from dairy to vegetable. In the mid-1990s, they became truck farmers, hauling their produce to markets. These days, Lupinski enjoys growing fresh local produce, and offering her neighbors, friends and community the chance to eat healthy fresh foods. Diana is especially known for her colored carrots - yellow, red, purple and, of course orange.

The growing trend toward local eating is healthy for her, for her fellow farmers, and for the economy of the local community. Plus, she says, buyers get the freshest and safest produce possible.

Diana and her husband, John, the "farming team," grew up here. They work the soil, make the decisions, and use minimal pesticides on their crops.

Marge Morales of Rock Tavern sees herself as a modern-day storyteller, using paint as her medium. In oils and watercolors, Marge offers more than images; her art tells stories that touch the heart and the soul.

Bounty Cookbook

POTATO SOUP
(courtesy of Diana Lupinski)

8 medium Yukon Gold potatoes, cubed
1 lg. onion or leek
4 oz. sour cream
4 oz. milk
1 TB. flour
1/2 stick margarine
salt and pepper

"Potatoes", by Steve Blumenthal .

In a 4 quart pot, place peeled potatoes and
just cover with water. Boil until tender. In
sauce pan sauté onion with margarine
until tender. When potatoes are tender,
mash slightly to desired consistency. In separate bowl, whip milk, sour cream and
flour until blended. Add salt and pepper to taste and pour into potatoes along with
onions. Cover and simmer 10 minutes and serve. * If serving again and the soup is
thick, add more milk. Yield 6 servings

"Noah Webster (of Webster's Dictionary,

Webster's Thesaurus, etc)

was the schoolmaster at Farmer's Hall Academy

(now Goshen Town Hall) in 1782. Schoolbooks were scarce

for a young country at war, so Webster

worked on a series of schoolbooks to give children

a uniquely American education."

Steve Blumenthal has been drawing and painting for over 20 years and his work is in many private collections. " I love to teach" he says,
"to give someone the tools and techniques to express themself" Steve is one of the founders of the Wallkill River School. He works in oils,
pastels, and watercolor.

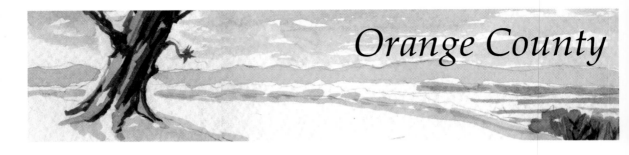

Sweet Basil
88 Route 17M
Harriman, NY   10926

John Piazza bought Sweet Basil restaurant in June 2007. A long established restaurant, it's small and intimate, with a quaint bar ideal for a before-dinner cocktail. It's a quiet restaurant, where you're comfortable dressed casually or elegantly. And the wait staff is particularly knowledgeable and capable.

For Piazza, the best part of running Sweet Basil is the joy of "presenting a dish of food that tastes so good!"

It's also important to use local ingredients - not just because of the freshness and the taste, but also because, as a small business, it's important to support other small businesses in the community. If everyone helps everyone, the cycle becomes complete, and prosperity is shared.

"Sweet Basil" by Bruce Thorne.

Piazza takes pleasure in greeting his clients and getting to know them, make them feel welcome. "We are a family-run establishment," he says, "and we care about our customers."

"Richard Ochs is one of Orange County's most talented native sons. Born in Newburgh in 1938, he remained in Orange County for most of his life, supplementing his art income with teaching. He grew to become an extremely sought-after workshop instructor and fine artist."

Bounty Cookbook

PASTA WITH VEAL AND TARRAGON-TOMATO CREAM SAUCE
(courtesy of John Piazza)

3 Tablespoon butter
4 Garlic cloves
1 lb Veal, ground (editor's note: ground turkey is a good substitute)
2 cups half and half
2 Tablespoons Tomato paste
1 teaspoon Tarragon
1 TableS lemon juice
3/4 teaspoon salt
1/4 teaspoon freshly ground pepper
1 (16oz) package of angel hair pasta, cooked

In a large skillet, melt butter over medium heat. Add crushed garlic cloves and saute until tender, about 1 minute. Add ground veal and saute until done, about 5 min.

Stire in half and half, tomato paste, tarragon, lemon juice, salt and pepper. Simmer until thick, about 10 minutes.

Serve pasta with the sauce and toss to mix evenly. Yield 6 servings

"George Washington gave the first
Purple Hearts medals to soldiers
in his Newburgh Headquarters in 1782.
Today we have a Purple Heart Hall of Fame Museum
in New Windsor to commemorate our courageous veterans."

Bruce Thorne-His style has been compared to Van Gogh for his rich color, thick impasto paint technique and his passion for painting.

S&SO Produce Farms
234 Mt. Eve Road
Goshen, NY

In the early 1900s, the Osczepinski family left Poland.
They came to America and found their way to the
Black Dirt region, where they started farming.

They're still farming today, still on that piece of land in
the Black Dirt.

Stanley Osczepinski is the farmer now. He's the the
third generation of Osczepinskis on the Goshen farm,
and is one of the founding members of the New York
City Greenmarket. He also brings produce to many
local Orange County farm markets.

"Snowman" by Pat Morgan

" Farmers have an undescribable pride in their profes-
sion," Osczepinski says. "To take a handful of seeds
and plant them in the ground and care for them until
they grow into vegetables is very gratifying. Not only because you are able to produce
something, but because you are feeding a community."

When the family gathers, he says, and the cook comes to the market because Grandpa loves
your tomatoes, or Auntie craves your corn, you feel great, Osczepinski says.

Eating locally gives people the freshest possible product, and keeps the local farmer
in business.

Osczepinski grows and brings to market 104 varieties of vegetables. "Because we are a locally based farm," he says, "our produce will be the freshest around. There is a less-than-
24-hour window from when our veggies are pulled from the ground and placed on our
market tables."

Pat Morgan, a watercolor painter, has studied with artists including Richard Ochs, Eli Rosenthal and Mel Stabin. Currently, she is
represented by the Wallkill River Gallery. She has received local and regional awards for her work, and enjoys teaching other painters
her love of watercolor.

Bounty Cookbook

PEANUT BUTTER CARROT CAKE
(courtesy of S+SO Produce Farms)

Cake
1 c. vegetable oil
2 c. white sugar
1/3 c. peanut butter
3 eggs
2 tsp. vanilla extract
2 c. shredded carrots
1 tsp. salt
1 c. bleached white flour
1 c. whole wheat flour
1 c. Bisquick
1/2 tsp. baking powder
1/2 tsp. cinnamon
1 c. raisins

Icing
8 oz. package cream cheese, softened
4 TB. butter, softened
1 tsp. vanilla
1 lb. box powdered sugar

"Carrots" by John Creagh

Preheat over to 350 degrees. Grease two 8 x2 round cake pans with vegetable shortening. Set aside. In a medium bowl sift together, white flour, whole wheat flour, Bisquick, baking soda, baking powder, cinnamon and salt. Set aside. In a large bowl mix vegetable oil, sugar, vanilla extract and peanut butter with an electric mixer on medium speed. Beat in eggs, when fully combined, add carrots and mix. On low, slowly beat in dry ingredients. Stir in raisins. Pour cake batter into the greased pans and bake for 30-35 minutes or until cake tester comes out clean. Cool completely before frosting.

For frosting, beat together cream cheese, butter and vanilla with an electric mixer on medium speed. When fully combined add powdered sugar at small increments until completely blended. Wait for cake to completely cool before icing.

John Creagh has been a painter and an instuctor for over 25 years, as well as a member and instructor for the Wallkill River School. His artwork is featured in many private colections around the world, you can visit him at www.jcreagh.com

Pine Island Spice Co.
64 County Route 12
Westtown, NY 10998

It was 1991, and Eileen Piascki-Couch was working as a research microbiologist at American Cyanamid. She was leaving her home at 6 in the morning and getting back at 6 at night. There was barely time to think, let alone plan and cook good meals for her family.

It was even tough to think good thoughts about some of the most familiar kitchen shortcuts. "It was impossible to find any soups or seasonings

"Logo", by Eileen Piasecki-Couch

without a ton of salt and artificial fillers," Piascki-Couch says. "So I started making them myself for my family and friends. And that was the beginning of Pine Island Herb & Spice."

For 15 years, she ran the business from her home. This past year, she moved to a commerical location, because she wanted to be able to do more. One goal was to include local blends with local ingredients, and add aline of organic herbs and blends.

Piascki-Couch says she learned to cook from her mother. Mom made everything from scratch, and was willing to try new things, experiment, take risks. That rubbed off on Piascki-Couch. "I love putting different flavors together, also," she says. "It seems like a natural thing to do."

One of the things she really enjoys is when potential customers taste her delicious wares and ask how much salt they contain, and she can tell them, "None!

The trend of eating and buying locally, Piascki-Couch says, helps people connect to their communities and their food sources. You can ask the farmer what's in the food. You can see where it's grown. That direct connection is like nothing else.

PUMPKIN CREAM CHEESE ROLL-UP
(courtesy of Pine Island Spice Co.)

3/4 cup flour
1 tsp. baking powder
3 1/2tsp Pine Island Herb and Spice Pumpkin Pie Spices
1/2 tsp. salt
3 eggs slightly beaten
1 cup sugar
2/3 cup cooked pumpkin or canned pumpkin
1 cup chopped walnuts

Filling
1 cup powdered sugar • 1 8 oz cream cheese • 6 TBS butter • 1 tsp. vanilla

Grease 15'x10'x1' pan, line with wax paper grease and flour paper.

Add the flour, baking powder pumpkin pie spice, and salt together. Set aside.

Whisk gently to mix all the ingredients. Beat the eggs and sugar till fluffy and thick. Beat in pumpkin. Stir in dry ingredients and and spread in lined pan evenly. Sprinkle the nuts evenly. Bake for 15 minutes at 375. Invert the cake onto a clean damp cloth dusted with powdered sugar, and peel off the waxed paper. Roll the cake and allow it to cool with the seam side down. Meanwhile, beat all the ingredients for the filling together until smooth. Leave at room temperature, until ready, about 1 hour. When the cake has cooled, unroll and spread the filling onto the roll. Reroll the cake without the towel and refrigerate until you are ready to serve. Dust with powdered sugar. Yield 6 servings

---

Piascki-Couch is proud of her business, and proud of her products. "I stand by them," she says, "with a 100% guarantee of quality and satisfaction."

Eileen Piasecki-Couch is owner and CEO of the Pine Island Herb & Spice Co. Inc. She is a wife, a mother of three boys, a former research microbiologist, an accomplished pilot who flies regularly, and an artist. She has been painting for the last 7 years, and has recently started selling her work. www.pineislandherb.com.

Maple Syrup

Maple Syrup Making is a traditional craft taught to us by Native Americans. Solar Installer Patrick Gallagher in Warwick is one of many home processors in Orange County that keeps the Maple Syrup flowing. Kenridge Farm at the Hudson Highlands Nature Museum in Cornwall offers Maple sugaring demonstrations in early Spring. Here's a few ideas of what you can do with local Maple syrup from the Maple Producers Association.

Sugar-on-Snow

This delicacy has been a traditional spring-time favorite at sugar houses and sugar camps for over 200 years. In some areas of the maple region, it is also known as "leather aprons" or "leather britches", due to its chewy, leathery consistency. In Orange County it is sugar-on-snow.

1/2 C. local Maple Syrup
A few inches of snow on the ground

Heat maple syrup to 22 to 28 degrees F. above the boiling point of water (234 degrees). The higher the heat the stiffer the candy! As soon as the syrup reaches the proper
temperature, it is poured or drizzled immediately, without stirring, over packed snow. Because it cools so rapidly, it will form a thin glassy, chewy, taffy-like sheet over the snow. Twirl it up with a fork and enjoy!

Maple-Glazed Butternut Squash

1 medium Butternut Squash, (seeded, quartered, cut into half-inch slices)
4 Tbsp. local Maple Syrup • 1/2Tsp. Ground Mace
4 Tbsp. Dark Rum • 2/3 C. Water

Place all ingredients in a large saucepan. Bring to a boil, then simmer for 15 minutes, or until the squash is tender. Reserving the cooking liquid, transfer the squash with a slotted spoon to a heated serving dish. Boil the cooking liquid until it is thickened, then pour it over the squash. Serves 4.

Maple Fudge

2 C. Local Maple Syrup • 1/2 C. Walnuts (chopped) • 1 Tbsp. Unsalted Butter
Candy thermometer • Tall sauce pan

Boil syrup and butter to 236 °F. Remove from heat and place in a pan of cold water. Stir vigorously until color begins to change, add walnuts. Pour into well-buttered 8" or 10" square pan. Cut into squares while still warm.

Farmers' Markets in Orange County
Courtesy of Orange County Tourism
www.OrangeCountyTourism.org
(845) 291-2136

Florida Farmers' Market Rt. 17A, across from Big V Shoprite HQ,
   Tuesday 10am - 4:30pm June 19 - October 9, 641-4482

Goshen Farmers' Market Village Square - Intersection of Main & Church Sts.
   Friday 10am - 5pm May 18 - October 26, 294-7741

Middletown Farmers' Market Erie Way from Grove St. to Cottage St.
   Saturday 8am - 1pm, June 16 - October 27, 343-8075

Monroe Farmers' Market Museum Village Parking lot, 1010 Rt. 17 M,
   Wednesday 9am - 3pm, June 22 - October 25, 344-1234

Newburgh/Downing Park Farmers' Market In Downing Park in Newburgh, near the corner
of South St. (NYS Rt. 52) & Robinson Ave. (Rt. 9W)
   Friday 10 AM - 5 PM, July 13 - October 26, 565-5559

Pine Bush Farmers' Market Parking lot at New & Depot Sts.
   Saturday 9am - 2pm, June 9 - October 20 , 744-6763

Tri State Farmers' Market Parking lot bet. Ball St. & Front St. in Port Jervis
   Saturday 8am - 2pm June 30 - October 27, 856-6694

Tuxedo Farmers' Market 240 Rt. 17 N. , Tuxedo Train Station
   Saturday 9am - 2pm, June 16 - October 27, 915-4058 ext.523

Walden Village Square Farmers' Market Fireman's Square next to Municipal Square in front
of Library & Village Square
   Thursday 12 Noon - 4 PM June 28 - October 25, 294-5557

Warwick Valley Farmers' Market, South St. parking lot, off Main St.,
   Sunday 9am - 2pm, May 20 - October 28, 987-9990

West Point/Town of Highlands Farmers' Market Municipal lot, Main Street near Visitors Ctr.
   Sunday 9am - 2:30pm June 24 – October28, 446-2459

This is the list of farms we contacted to be in the cookbook. These farms retail directly to the Orange County public. There are many we probably missed. Call the farm for hours. (C.S.A. means you pay a flat rate up front for a weekly share of the harvest.)

Abundant Life Farm, 168 Prospect Rd. Middletown, 692-3550, Biodynamic vegetables, cheese, wool

Acorn Hill, Goat cheese, at Pine Bush Farmer's Market

Applewood Winery, 82 Four Corners Rd. Warwick, 988-9292 vineyard

Bellvalle Farms Creamery, 385 Route 17A, Warwick, www.bellvalefarms.com 988-1818 ice cream

BenMarl Vineyard 156 Highland Ave. Marlboro-on-Hudson, vineyard www.benmarl.com

Bialas Farm, Goshen Farmers Market, vegetables www.Bialasfarms.com

Blooming Hill Farm, 1251 Route 208, Washingtonville 782-7310 Organic C.S.A., farm store, cafe

Brotherhood Winery, 100 Brotherhood Plaza, Washingtonville, 496-3661, www.Brotherhoodwinery.net

Cassano Farms, Middletown, Caterina 342-0809

C.Rowe & Sons, 113 Station Rd. Campbell Hall, 427-2254, vegetables, x-mas trees, hay

Dagele Brothers Produce, Florida Farmer's Market

D'Attalico Organic Farm Mission Land Rd.Pine Island, 258-7451,Warwick Farmer's Market

Destination Farm, 26 Flourescent Dr. Slate Hill, NY 355-2651

Eldred, Todd, Ward. Ave. Chester, 469 3585 beef

Frank Hoeffner Farm, farm stand on Route 211 near O.C. Airport, Montgomery, vegetables, fruits

Froehlich's Farm, farm stand on Albany Post Road, Montgomery, vegetables

Four Winds Farm, 158 Marabac Rd., Gardiner, 255.3808, Polly Armour, C.S.A., poultry, eggs, meats

Hoeffner Farm, 405 Goodwill Rd., Montgomery, farm stand with vegetables, fruits, plants, flowers.

Hodgson's Farm, Albany Post Rd. and Route 52 in Montgomery, vegetables, pumpkins, tourism.

Harmony Farm, 144 Broadlea Rd. Goshen, 294-3181 organic C.S.A.

JADS Farm Market, 641 Route 1, Pine Island, 258-1102, vegetables, eggs

John Lupinski Farm, 1 Houston Rd. Goshen, 361-1429 vegetables

Jones Farm, 190 Angola Rd. Cornwall, 534-4445; farm store open year round, petting zoo, frame shop

Kiernan Farm, 1308 Brunswick Road, Gardiner, 255-8998, Bed & Breakfast, beef farm

Kitchen Gourmet, Florida farmer's market, Alice Zis 651-4116

Lynnhaven Farm, 414 Church Rd, Pine Bush, 744-6089 goat cheese & milk

Lawrence Farms & Orchards, 39 Colandrea Rd. Newburgh, 562-4268,
       www.lawrencefarmsorchards.com

Maskers Apple Orchard, 45 Ball Rd.Warwick, 986-8852, www.maskers.com farm store

Midsummer Farm, 156 E. Ridge Rd., Warwick, 986-9699, www.midsummerfarm.com
       C.S.A., meat

Morgiewicz Produce, 406 Pulaski, Goshen

Ochs Orchards, 4 Ochs Lane, Warwick, 986-1591, farm store, fruit, vegetables, eggs, jams,
       maple

O'Dells Farm, 176 Millsburg Rd., Middletown, 355-7916, meats, eggs

Overlook Farm Market, Route 9W, Middlehope, 562-5780 farm store, vegetables, fruits

Pennings Farm Market, 161 Route 94,Warwick, 986-1059, www.penningsfarmmarket.com
       farm store

Philles Bridge Farm Project, 45 Philles Bridge Rd, Gardiner, NY 256-9108,
       www.philliesbridge.org C.S.A.

Pine Hill Farm, 3298 Route 94, Chester, 325-1115, fruit, vegetables, flowers, herbs, breads

Roe's Orchard, 3278 Route 94, Chester, 469-4724, farm store, vegetables, fruits, cider,
       honey, flowers

Royal Acres, 621 Scotchtown-Collabar Rd, Scotchtown, 692-6719;
       Pine Bush Farmer's Market

S&SO Produce Farm, 234 Mt. Eve Rd.,Goshen, 651-4211; Florida/Monroe/Goshen
       Farmer's Markets

Scattered Acres Farm, Meadow Avenue, Chester 469-4549

Scheuermann Farms, 73 Little York Rd.,Warwick, 258-4221, vegetables, herbs, honey,
       flowers, jams

Slate Hill Orchards, 258 Route 6, Slate Hill, 355-4493, farm store, fruit, vegetables, dairy,
       eggs, breads

Soons Orchards, 23 Soons Circle, New Hampton, 374-5471, www.soonsorchards.com
       farm store

Sugar Loaf Mountain Herbs, 1361 Main. St., Sugar Loaf, 469-6460, fresh herbs, teas, plants

Sycamore Farms,1851 Route 211 East, Wallkill, NY, 692-2684, C.S.A., farm stand

Walnut Grove Farm, 235 Youngblood Road, Montgomery, 313-4855,
       www.WalnutGroveFarms.com store/CSA

Warwick Valley Winery 114 Little York Rd, Warwick, 258-4858, www.wwinery.com

W. Rogowski Farm, 329 Glenwood Road, Pine Island, 258-4423 www.rogowskifarm.com
       store/C.S.A.

Orange County ShopRites:

ShopRite of Wallkill
400 Route 211 East - Wallkill Plaza
Middletown, NY 10940
(845)342-2103Mon-Fri 6am-1am
Sat 6am-1am
Sun 6am-1am

ShopRite of Newburgh
88 North Plank Road Suite 1
Newburgh, NY 12550
(845)561-9420Mon-Fri 7am-12am
Sat 7am-12am
Sun 7am-10pm

ShopRite of Middletown
125 Dolson Avenue
Middletown, NY 10940
(845)343-1139Mon-Fri 6am-1am
Sat 6am-1am
Sun 6am-1am

ShopRite of Chester Plaza
78 Brookside Avenue Suite 122
Chester, NY 10918
(845)469-7400Mon-Fri 6am-12am
Sat 6am-12am
Sun 6am-10pm

ShopRite of Montgomery
99 Hawkins Drive
Montgomery, NY 12549
(845)457-4114Mon-Fri 7am-12am
Sat 7am-12am
Sun 7am-10pm

ShopRite of Monroe
Route 17 M - ShopRite Plaza
Monroe, NY 10950
(845)783-4496Mon-Fri 6am-1am
Sat 6am-1am
Sun 6am-1am

ShopRite of Vailsgate
Route 32
Vails Gate, NY 12584
(845)863-1051Mon-Fri 6am-1am
Sat 6am-1am
Sun 6am-1am

ShopRite of Warwick
153 South Route 94
Warwick, NY 10990
(845)987-1200Mon-Fri 6am-12am
Sat 6am-12am
Sun 6am-10pm